THE20PROJECT

A collection of stories, wisdom and advice from life on the other side of 20.

Hilary A. Curry

Halston Publishing

North Vancouver

PUBLISHED BY HALSTON PUBLISHING

http://www.halstonpublishing.com

Library and Archives Canada Cataloguing in Publication

Curry, Hilary

The20Project

Issued in print and electronic formats

ISBN 978-0-9938876-2-8 Paperback

ISBN 978-0-9938876-0-4 Hard Cover

ISBN 978-0-9938876-4-2 .mobi

ISBN 978-0-9938876-3-5 .epub

ISBN 978-0-9938876-1-1 .pdf

1. Literary Collections: Essays 2. Biography & Autobiography: General 3. Self-Help: Motivational & Inspirational

The20Project Logo Design: Ryan Caputo

Book Cover Design: Bridge Braun

CONTENTS

PROJECT CONTRIBUTORS

Alma Kenup
Amberley Laverick
David Mitchell
Flavio Kenup
Heather Stafford
Hilary Curry
Juan Rodriguez
Julia Kerrigan
Margaret Ebrecht
Michelle Arduini
Nancy Jean Lahn
Nicola Holden
Robert Jaques
Russell Cullingworth
Sandie Atkinson
Sébastien Lacour
Shannon Teemull
Stephanie Alexander
Terri Lyons Taiaroa
Tosh Hattori

PREFACE

Every project starts with an idea. This project was conceived on the 1st of January 2014 and was a result of more than one mentoring conversation with young adults who were lost in life or making bad decisions as a result of too many choices; they needed advice on how to get through their 'quarter-life crisis.'

So, I registered the domain, built a site and sent out a Facebook request to 50 of my closest friends who might want to participate in the project; and 6 months, 20 contributors and countless hours of work later…

VOILA! We have a book.

This book is about journeys. The contributors were asked to write a chapter to share their wisdom with 20-year-olds, and the exercise has been as much a reflective one as a sharing one for the contributors.

However, we hope that anyone of any age will learn from the stories contained within these pages and put that new knowledge to good use. We also aspire to make a bit of a profit that we can donate to Makomborero to help kids who otherwise wouldn't have the opportunity. Makomborero is a Zimbabwe based charity that supports a select group of high potential kids every year through their A-Levels. These kids go on to earn scholarships at universities such as McGill and Dartmouth. The poem "I am potential" was penned by one of these students.

Although I am the founder of this project, I wouldn't have gotten anywhere without support, input and expertise from many amazing people listed on the next page.

From the bottom of my heart, I thank you and dedicate this book to you.

Love, Hilary

WITH THANKS

The Contributors — without you there would be no book! Thank you for putting up with my demands and seeing this project through to the end. I know it hasn't been easy!

Theresa Laviolette — you're an editing angel.

Trena White from Page Two — thank you for getting the project from edit to print with your pearls of advice on the industry!

Steve Rosenberg & the crew at Pull Focus — you guys are magic.

Our marketing video participants — thank you for showing up; you are very much appreciated!

Ryan Caputo — you are really the jack-of-all-trades.

Bridget Braun – you are truly our graphic design guru! Thanks for coming in at the last min to help with the book cover and posters.

Carla Beak — thank you for the feedback & summary.

My parents — thank you for always telling it to me straight (especially when I don't want to hear it) – Love you!

All of our Kickstarter supporters — you guys made this book a reality.

I AM POTENTIAL

...So they told me I can't be...
they reigned their opinion upon my shoulders...
weight unshakable...
reason unfathomable...
nonetheless destructive...
their eyes made me stare into the abyss...
searching in the hope that I see my worth...
maybe I could at least find a penny worth of freedom
from this...
from this face of scrutiny and discover my potential...
and in their opinion...
if I even had any...
but am I bound at the bowels of worthlessness...
is this my portion...
is this why I get up every morning...
to scrub their feet and watch them as they step on my face as
they aspire to what their soul so chooses...
have I no humanity left in me that they don't see me as a living being,
a fellow peer who wants to thrive and discover the meaning of life...
Have the gods spat at the very face of my existence
that I should find no peace...
no destiny...
forsaken, alone...

Have I no potential...
Mother, oh mother have I no potential...

Answer me walls, you have seen my pain...
always around as I slipped my body in between the
dark shade you provided...
hiding my shame from them...answer me damn it...
do you also side with them...
the reason you stay quiet as they abuse and torture me,
my spirit wails and you watch, have I no potential...
Have I no potential...
have I no potential...
Weep my soul weep...
for this is the last time you weep...
you are what I am ...
I am what I chose...
no longer shall I stand for your approval...
shall I tolerate your stares...
Shall I see you as elite and myself a doormat where
you wipe and rub the dirt away...
I am strong...
I am what I am...
special in my difference...
read my lips as they dance to tell you this...

I AM POTENTIAL...

by Ryan Maponga
Makomborero Student

ALMA

As my 28th year of life rapidly approaches, I feel the need to reflect during this milestone year. It's been almost two decades since I received the greatest life advice. As you can imagine, at eight years old, I didn't have even an inkling of what was being gifted to me.

The day was like many others. I sat in the passenger seat of my grandpa's old-man Lincoln Town Car. I continued to politely crane my neck in my grandfather's direction even though the too-big seatbelt kept uncomfortably rubbing at the nape of my neck and kept unfairly pressing on my right shoulder. I tugged at my constraints as I pretended to listen to yet another lecture from Grandpa Morris. As he carried on about god-knows-what, my eyes stayed momentarily locked on his face, though his eyes kept distractingly flitting back and forth between Los Angeles traffic and me.

For the split seconds that his eyes returned to the road, I kept sneaking glances at his old, craggy hands—the only source of entertainment for me as I sat in his musty car, surrounded by the lulling orchestral styling of Mozart on the radio. I compared Grandpa's hands to my smooth, caramel-colored hands and wondered what would happen to me in life to one day land me with hands like his, weirdly angular, speckled and barely resembling what I examined on myself. It was the dull moments like these that made me wish that I were an adult already; mostly so I could punctuate the conversation (or soliloquy, as it were) with my own relevant thoughts and be seen as insightful instead of as naïve and rude.

Those hands, along with the smell of newspapers, pastrami sandwiches and the comforting stench of lox and cream cheese on just-warmed onion bagels, are the greatest thing I have to remember Grandpa Morris by. After hours spent finding amusement in those hands, I was an expert on them. I found wonder in the long, thin fingers that seemed to have rebelliously grown hooked with the passage of time. Hands shouldn't look like that, I was sure. The most pronounced feature on those giant, ancient hands was the liver spots, as dark-colored as the name suggested. After car ride upon car ride spent thinking it through, I decided the liver spots best bore a striking resemblance to the freckles on Baby Sinclair's cheeks (of "Not the momma!" *Dinosaurs* fame). I wondered how they came about and if there was any way to erase them. As I contemplated how the spots of this old man were related to the hilarious prehistoric TV family I loved so much, my grandpa sent me reeling by waving his palm in front of my face and croaking, "Are you listening to me?"

I quickly wiped the goofy smile off my face (the one that creeps on whenever I'm thinking about something I find particularly funny) and stammered back, "Grandpa, in ten years I'll be 18. I won't have to sit in this car anymore! I'll be an adult and I'll be able to do as I please!"

Grandpa, offended by my gall, looked away from me and kept his eyes fixed on the cars filing by. The expression on his face was as solemn as it had been moments before.

As we approached a red light, he turned to me, waved a pointed finger two inches away from my nose and quietly muttered through gritted teeth, "Listen to me. This is very important." Pause. "Whatever you do. Don't. Get. Old!" I faintly remember a smirk on my grandfather's face.

Wha-? Oh, great! I thought. I left my *Dinosaurs* daydream for this! Don't get old? Is this the kind of silly nonsense I'll be doling out when I'm old, too? Get me out of this car! Adulthood, come fast!

Ten years later, at the awkward trappings of eighteen, life started to get dizzyingly complicated. I hated being an adult. There were taxes and life-goals, a weirdly ironic thing called maturity, bills, insurance of sorts, deadlines, real homework, penny-paying part-time jobs, and there was impossibly expensive college tuition. The question, "What do you want to be when you grow up?" didn't seem so fantastically magical now. It was anxiety-inducing and noxious.

As my mind became boggled by the business of being an adult, I desperately wished I could turn back the dial of time. I began to reflect on the ramblings-on of my grandfather. Maybe the old man was on to something. But how do you go about not getting old? It's not exactly a choice you make. Like the liver spots that appeared on his hands, getting old is something that inevitably happens with the passage of time. Still, his words sat in the back of my mind, dancing around teasingly as I grappled with the misery of adulthood. What would I do with my life?

Twenty came and went. Twenty-one came and went. I graduated college, enrolled in grad school and like the good little Mexican immigrant daughter that I was, I not only met, but exceeded, my parents' expectations of me. I was wretchedly unhappy. I would have traded a diploma in a heartbeat to be able to be chauffeured around like in my youth, with only unkempt hair requiring my attention.

When I was 22, my grandfather became gravely ill. The cancer in his liver, which he had found out about only weeks before, had metastasized to his kidneys and in a blur of a few months he transformed from a jovial, pot-bellied, permanently smiling old man to a waif-looking human being, with his skin hanging from his bones like poorly tailored, oversized clothing. I loved my grandfather dearly and I happily drove through the two hours of horn-blaring, rush-hour traffic to see him at the hospital. I would force a smile as I walked to his room, refusing to believe he looked as bad as the last time. Surely he's put on weight now! I lied. Surely things are looking up. People recover from cancer all the time, right?

I would show up with a case of Ensure, as requested by my grandmother. As soon as I rounded the corner to his room, I had to quickly avert my gaze to the floor. Each time I wished that the patient before me was the wrong one. His dishevelled, starved-looking state caused a lump to creep up in my throat, knocked the wind out of me, and left me stunned. It was the same every time. I would fight back tears as I would muster enough courage to lift my stare from the ground to look at my grandfather in the face. When I was met with that lifeless stare, I had to anchor my own eyes to the only part of him that resembled what I always knew, his hands. Still sinewy and featuring more signs of life than the rest of him, his hands helped me gain my composure. These were our visits. Occasionally I would manage to squeak out, "How are you?" I was a wimp.

On one particular visit, I managed to keep my eyes locked on my grandfather's face for a long time. It was the visit I will most remember because it was the day I finally learned the meaning of his enigmatic words.

This visit was different because as I drove to the hospital, I rounded the streets to give myself more time to mentally prepare for our encounter. This time I would not choke. As I pep-talked myself, I noticed a deli sign flashing out of the corner of my eye. Instinctively, I pulled in and sat in the parking lot. I really wasn't ready for the hospital today. Not now. After sitting in my car for 20 minutes, I got out, headed for the counter and ordered myself two sandwiches; they were pastrami. I'm pretty sure my grandfather was not allowed to eat this for many reasons, but whatever. I knew he wouldn't turn down real food after only being allowed hospital-fare and old-people formula.

When I entered my grandfather's room, my grandmother cringed as she saw the grease seep through the brown paper bag I carried; I was definitely not going to be making this delivery without protest. Surprisingly, she said nothing. I shuffled over to my grandfather's bed and without any words, handed the bag over. As he opened the contents of the grease-saturated case, his eyes glistened with fresh tears and a smile began to form at the corners of his mouth. There he was; the man I had known all my youth. It was the smile my grandfather would wear when we sat in the car together, after he felt he had told a particularly clever pun, "Point to your head and abbreviate mountain!" That smile. It was the smile a child wears every day when they find amusement in all of the wondrous things in the world. It was the smile I wore the day I thought of how much I loved the cast of *Dinosaurs*. In that instance, it was all clear. The epiphany I had been waiting on for years finally happened. Don't get old.

Those three words finally made sense. I understood Grandpa Morris to mean don't let yourself get caught up in the whirlwind of misery that can sometimes characterize life, especially life surrounding adulthood. He meant that you need to let yourself be driven by the passion deeply buried within the quirky eight-year-old version of yourself. On that long-ago day, during that car ride, Grandpa feared for my eight-year-old spunk as he noted that I often spoke of yearning for the adulthood that was talked up so much. Don't get old. Like letting yourself get fat after college, or letting yourself get lazy in a relationship, the getting isn't inevitable. Age can't be helped, sure, but the desire to be the version of yourself that the child in you would be proud of is something to aspire to.

After my grandfather passed away, I decided that the best way to honor his memory was to live my life with his words as a guideline. Before I made that decision, I felt every day was characterized by the same uncomfortable feeling a child has when restrained by an ill-fitting seatbelt. It was that feeling tenfold. I felt suffocated and trapped; but since I noticed others around me felt the same, I didn't question the culture. Once I let myself be free of the harness of expectations surrounding my actions, however, the youthful joy I so longed for came once more. I did an about-face on the career that was chosen for me and instead I let myself be driven by my own unconventional ambitions. As I near 28, I realize that grandpa would be proud. I have my dream job; I live in as exotic a place as I could have ever thought up; I am happy—and I have him to thank for advising me well all those years ago.

I've done well to hold onto the youthful verve that characterized eight-year-old me, as Grandpa Morris had intended. For one, I've embraced the wanderlust that has plagued me since before I could accurately point to countries on a globe. Since I've been able to earn money on my own, I've been on the move. When I turned 15, my parents insisted on a *Quinceanera,* a Mexican rite-of-passage party, while I begged instead for half the money that it would take to fund the party so I could go to Rome. They thought it was a joke. After years of watching me flit about this planet, they realize that I was serious.

I met my husband in Abu Dhabi when I took the first job in my chosen career as a teacher. He didn't speak a lick of English and I had never heard a word uttered in Brazilian Portuguese. Guess who offered English lessons? Over the last few years, we've created a bi-cultural polyglot family. We often have ourselves some good belly-busting laughs from the confusion that comes with having so many cultures and languages to keep in check, but I wouldn't have it any other way.

I am certainly not advocating that everyone make the same life choices that I have made; detailing the way my life has gone since allowing myself to lead a life outside of the prescribed norm simply serves to illustrate Grandpa Morris' theory of living a life infused with our youthful dreams.

The nugget of advice I have to pass along to others is exactly what my grandfather told me: Don't get old. Although to his goal of keeping a youthful vivacity I would also add a caveat of not letting things in your life get old. Do what moves you, and if a shade of dullness overcomes what once was exciting, change it up! You might just find yourself in a foreign land, challenging your preconceived notions of the way the world works. Who knows?

AMBERLEY

Remember, as a child, when we believed
ourselves to be the tallest,the smartest,
the most wonderful creature to ever exist?
Each scrawled drawing, a masterpiece.
Each story scribed, a classic.

Those moments breathed,
moved the space where our hearts lay.
They played outside in the autumn,
tossing dried colour into blue skies.
Alive, they danced on floor boards,
drank milk from the carton,
until they were shaken. Bruised. Violated.

Told not enough good, not enough pretty,
not enough intelligent,
not enough, never enough.

Now we must reclaim those moments.
Find a reality from within.
If we reach inside, through the soup of disillusionment,
there will lay nothing truer than that small child,
the one we abandoned but who never left.
She just sat about,
building a castle with pebbles of memory.

She will smile. With a voice, as soft as marshmallows,
she will ask,"Shall we play?"

Taking your hand, gently,
she will lead you around yourself,
unfolding ideas that you hid away in drawers
you thought to be jammed shut.

She will tumble them out,
carefully arranging each one,
creating whole universes that
time had squashed.

Pointing, the gurgle of her voice will exclaim,
'That one! That one would work perfectly,
if only we had a unicorn.'

Can you hear her laughter, chiming in your ears?

I write prose and poetry. Never do I write about myself. Therefore, this is as much about sharing my story as it is a personal challenge.

As my thirties edge me forward, constantly I hear of people—grown-up people—unhappy with where their lives are. These are invariably those who followed the crowd. By never stepping back and learning who they are, what drives them, what sparks passion, they all trod the well-worn path. Reasons tend to be numerous, but fear often plays a large part. A realisation is dawning upon them, and many are afraid it is too late to make changes, or believe themselves to be trapped by their choices.

The tale I find myself a part of follows no script. Regret does not visit my days and fear knocks on my door only when I am about to throw myself off the edge of a cliff into the unknown. And that is a fantastic feeling.

How, then, do you or I or the guy next to you on the bus end up where we do?

Life is a series of events that come into being from decisions we make, which are influenced by both our environment and innate attributes. This may come across as an over-simplified explanation of a complex world; however it is my explanation, for my world, that works for me.

As a child I was brash, bossy, confident, independent and terribly self-righteous. Due to circumstances of one variety or another I was never under any pressure from my parents to take a particular direction in life. As a teenager I picked my own school subjects, joined extracurricular activities because I wanted to, worked, played and generally enjoyed not being told what to do.

A combination of my personality and upbringing allowed me to see the world as mine for the taking. At 18, I dropped out of university and, packing my bags, left Australia, with no knowledge of which track I would meander down.

So many times during this period of my life people would say to me, "You are so lucky!" Believe me; luck had nothing to do with how my life was progressing. I was not born into money, was never handed a golden plane ticket. My warts were visible. I often fell down; I cried and stamped my feet like a princess. I did not always sleep with my mind in restful dreams. Quite literally, I had absolutely no idea what I was doing. I just knew I was living.

This time abroad was laced with an awareness that I was looking for a focus; a passion or interest that would lead me back to study. Though I never put a time limit on when this would happen.

Whilst in London I worked as a nanny. Here I experienced, for the first time, the absolute joy in realising that another human being now knew something, and would know it for the rest of their lives, because I had helped them. There is something incredibly powerful in the transfer of knowledge from one to another. I decided to become a teacher.

Four and a half years had passed. I returned home.

Throughout university I was ferocious in my quest to learn. Real-world experience with children meshed perfectly with academic explanations of behaviours I had encountered, and ideas formed from my own observations. I also realised I had no desire to teach in the mainstream education system. For me, university was creating graduates expected to slide into predefined jobs. Frustration grew as I tried to push against these expectations.

Once the degree was completed many thought I would find a job, marry my boyfriend, mortgage my life and buy a dog. However, now armed with new-found knowledge, it was the perfect time to venture back out into the world. For 12 months I pottered. Then it was time to find a "proper" job. Back to London I went.

Let me take a moment to discuss goals. Goals are great. In my very early twenties it was returning to study. Following that was having a solid notion of how I wanted to spend my work days by the time I reached 30. Loose goals, yet still very important milestones to be working towards; set the boundaries but allow total freedom within.

At this point I was hurtling into the tail end of decade number three. Thirty was approaching.

"Proper" job hunting tired me. Even though I had always danced to my own tune, I still very much felt the pressure of the everyday world eying me up, waiting for me to tumble, perhaps come crawling back to the "real" world. However, my inner voice always sang loudest. With a proper job still in sight, I decided to do things my way. I took a job beneath my skill set and volunteered at an organisation I wanted to work for. Three months later I signed the contract for my very first permanent job, as a literacy teacher for underprivileged and vulnerable young people. I was just about to turn 29.

The job lasted one year.

I was miserable.

I quit.

Staying in London, I took temporary teaching work (solidifying my thoughts on mainstream education), hinted at starting a business, rediscovered my passion for writing and took a massive pay cut.

I was blissfully happy.

Whilst employed in my grown-up job, I had been unwillingly dragged into setting up a creative writing group that was being funded by another organisation and facilitated by a Ghanaian writer. I knew I was going to quit my job; however, I took on the project.

I am proud to say it was a huge success. Once I left my job, along with an ex-colleague I continued to facilitate the group for another year. We worked with various organisations, hosted spoken-word events and I set up another writing group separately. I networked and built something meaningful.

There is a lesson here about saying yes, when all you want to do is eat your lunch in peace and not be asked to join a meeting with someone you immediately judge to be of no value to your future, and who then becomes a pivotal character in your story and a great friend.

However, in early 2013 I grew restless. I knew this feeling. After staying put for three years I had achieved much, felt secure and comfortable. It was not enough. I walked away and moved to Kenya.

Kenya was interesting. A part of the world I knew nothing about taught me more about humanity than I thought possible. But I could not settle. Cogs were turning and churning, leading to restless nights and early mornings drinking tea and watching the ducks multiply with each sunny day.

After 13 years of moving and trying and testing and generally seeing what is out there, I had made a decision. I knew where I wanted to be and it was not Kenya.

How did that happen?

It happened because I had taken time to learn who I am. Over the years, spending ridiculous amounts of time by myself had enabled me to focus inward. I know how my brain works, why I behave in certain ways, what I like and what I do not like. Because I have created myself, I am completely comfortable with WHO I AM. And along the way I have found that place in the world that fits me. That place is not where I was born or where I grew up or went to school. It is a place found because I went looking, refusing to settle for not quite good enough.

It is in this place I am parked now. Newly arrived and, as at other times when I have decided to wrench safety and comfort from my life, absolutely terrified. When that particular brand of fear raises itself though, I know I have made the correct choice.

This is part one of my story. No one on this Earth has this story except me. And no one else in this world has yours. Do not allow others to own your story or force you to duplicate theirs.

"But I want to play amongst the stars!"

How do you explain to a small child that we cannot?
How can you encourage the young to reach for
those same stars when we are
limited to the regions of our own planet?

We are boxed in.
Prisoners of an atmosphere that sustains life;
one we are rapidly poisoning
with the filth of human construction.

I want to go beyond the train tracks but I fail to find a land
untainted by metal and concrete,
assembled into responsible shapes.

Wanting more, seeking more but
always finding the same,
I begin to turn inwards.
In here there are doors that have yet to be built;

whole colonies of creatures only now hunting for light.
No rules as these would melt the beauty.
Everything is fragile but reflections radiate
strength that softly mists windows
with the breath of newly born ideas.

We do not repeat in here but borrow,
expand, embellish.
Chase, yet never follow.
No one ever drives themselves
over and over and over into a brick wall.
We have all mastered the art of steering.

Don't be fooled, though, by the enchanted,
because with any tale of magical lands there is
Horror. Betrayal. Ugliness.
Poisoned apples; gingerbread houses;
rings of untold power.

That is the fun of it. The battle: good versus evil.
I send in an army of misfit fairies,
only to retreat due to an onslaught of broken visions,
dressed in jewel-encrusted armour,
wielding shards of common expectation.
This allows me though to use the fairies as decoys
while top-hatted pelicans begin their overhead assault.

Playing amongst the stars, perhaps not;
but the universes locked inside
our own selves are so limitless,
what cannot be touched by our hands
can be danced with in our souls.

So next time a small child asks the impossible,
pretend, for a time,
that here on Earth these things exist.

Push boundaries over the norm, the everyday,
the moments that occur and occur and occur,
lacking thought and colour.
Scratch the edge of purpose,
tear back that peeling wallpaper,
and rip up loose floorboards.

There will never be an answer
and that is our solution.
Tomorrow is never the end point.
After comes only more tomorrows
that need to be filled with invention and tea parties,
silly hats and dancing under the sun and,
if you are lucky,
playing amongst the stars of your own creation.

DAVE

Reflecting some 30 years later on your twenties, and trying to make some sort of sense out of that chaotic time of life, is no easy task. Memories become faded around the edges, disappointments lose their sharpness and successes are magnified in the unreliable glow of nostalgia. My twenties were mainly spent during the 1980s—a time of dubious fashion, big hair and questionable taste in music.

In your twenties life looks as though it will go on forever. Of course, there were older people around all the time, parents and grandparents, for instance; people got sick, some passed on, but at that age all the bad things seemed to happen to someone else. I'd assumed that my life would be nicely compartmentalized and follow a fairly predictable path. Back then, it was a time to travel and have fun. I thought that later on there would be time enough for marriage, some kids probably, a steady job, nice house (well a mortgage at least) and hopefully a degree of financial, social and emotional stability before slowing right down and putting my feet up—a nice early retirement and maybe some travel to compensate for all that sacrifice.

Of course, it didn't quite work out like that. Life, it would appear, is what actually happens to you while you are busy making all those unrealized plans.

Not only has the wind blown me further afield and for much longer than I could ever have imagined, but it's done so at a quite terrifying rate of knots. I turned 50 recently, but it seems just yesterday that I was right in the middle of my very own "roaring twenties." Fortunately, it's also been a lot more fun and a lot more interesting than I might have expected and, on reflection, it wasn't such a bad time to live through after all.

Economic uncertainties, global environmental issues and the many other pressing concerns facing those in their twenties today make me realize the opportunities that were open to me back then, and that I might also have actually picked up a few tricks along the way. You'll often hear people say, "If I knew then what I know now...," which is, of course, impossible to recapture; but I do know now what I didn't know then, and that could be just as instructive for young people facing the same kinds of decisions and life choices I had all those, very short, years ago.

When looking back and thinking about how my attitudes and outlook on life have constantly evolved over the years, it's probably best to start at the beginning and go back to childhood. You wouldn't think about it at the time, but those formative experiences go a long way to shaping the adult you become.

My own upbringing was far from privileged, but nor was it in any way deprived. My mum was completely devoted to raising both my sister and I even though she was a single woman during the less tolerant seventies—no easy task! We didn't have a lot of money, but got by on a lot of love and plenty of laughter.

One of the most defining moments of my young life came one day in 1969 when I was six years old. I was in the backyard chasing dragons and rescuing damsels in distress when my dad came outside, said he was going to go on a business trip and kissed me goodbye. We were never to see him again. To this day he remains listed as a missing person, suspected of having been murdered in a small, out-of-the-way town in south-western New South Wales by the name of Griffith. Not an auspicious end. At that time Griffith was a hotbed of Australian mafia activity, and I was to find out years after that my dad had something of a gambling problem. The combination of factors left little to the imagination. There were unconfirmed reports and stories (occasional innuendo) over the years saying that he had been sighted here or there, or just about anywhere and everywhere, but nothing concrete was ever heard from him again.

As a child, you simply adapt and move on; it's not as though you have any choice in the matter. Children have very little choice and virtually no influence on what befalls them when they are growing up. In the end, it's how you deal with the setbacks and negative experiences that defines you and hopefully moves you forward.

In the immediate context of The20Project, readers may wonder if my less-than-standard life and lifestyle has been influenced by not having a male role model around during my formative years. Who knows? Maybe; maybe not. I don't suppose I will ever really know. I guess I could find out from a psychologist, but I have never felt the need to ask. One thing is for sure; it affected my sister and me in totally different ways. She is a devout Catholic and a devoted mother to 11 fantastic kids, is enjoying a long and happy marriage and has never felt the urge to ever set foot outside Australia. Conversely, I'm a single man, an atheist, and a frenetic traveller. Yet, we also love each other to death, despite the many differences. Go figure, as they say!

So how did a small boy from New South Wales end up at 50 in the Middle East? Most full-time expatriates usually want to live beyond normal expectations, and enjoy dealing with vastly different and varied cultures. The path to my present situation probably started in 1984 with another journey. That seems a long time ago these days; yet also as if it were yesterday.

Back then, it was supposed to be a once-in-a-lifetime trip. A three-week trip transformed itself—with a little help from me—into a year-long working "holiday" in London, interspersed with regular hops over to the European continent. There is nothing particularly unusual in young Australians spending a year or two overseas; in fact it is almost a rite of passage. I was fortunate enough to meet a selection of people who quickly showed me that my life in small-town Australia was a very insular one indeed. Suddenly friendly discussions were about the political situations in Africa, apartheid and the Cold War; world music and crazy festivals were suddenly on the agenda. It would be a very different young man who returned to Australia.

Most young Aussies return home determined not to let the travel passion die out, but inexorably the memories fade and it becomes time to put "childish" things behind and get on with the real business of starting a family, putting down the mortgage deposit and settling down.

For me, though, the fire never really did die; it just flickered away in the background as I bought into "the great Australian dream" of a home on a quarter acre and all the security that supposedly brings.

I threw myself into sporting pursuits and a 12-year career playing part-time rugby league. Add a dog and a cat to the mixture and I was living in a suburban nirvana. I kind of assumed that this was to be my lot. However, a great Australian tradition called "long service leave" changed all that. Long service leave is available to an employee after ten years continuous service with the same employer and comprises three months fully paid leave. I simply tacked an extra two weeks onto my usual four weeks leave, dug out the old backpack and started to get excited about travelling again during my holidays over the next few years.

First up, I headed for Thailand to stay with an old friend who was then living, working and researching at Chang Mai University. It was this trip, more than any other, that opened my eyes to new possibilities—possibilities that would have lain dormant but for my friend, his inspirational partner, and all the people I met through them.

Suddenly a simple irrigation specialist from Wagga Wagga was mixing with, and helping out, human rights activists in Thailand; meeting advocates for indigenous groups; and being photographed by rather sinister-looking agents of the Myanmar/Burmese government—the plight of refugees from Myanmar/Burma being very high on the agenda at that time.

It all seemed a lot more vital, important and consequential than walking the dog and watering the plants back home. I was surrounded by inspirational people whose passion for their work and lives was contagious. Yet, without a niche of my own I once again returned home and started to look out for an opportunity not just to travel, but to move overseas and to go and live in one of these exotic locations on a more long-term basis. The possibility of expatriate life had wormed itself firmly back into my brain. My holidays in the ensuing few years followed a similar tack: head to Asia and immerse myself in short hops into Southeast Asia from my base in Chang Mai, becoming desperately, insanely envious of the lives my friends were leading over there.

By 2006, I had had enough. I simply could not find a way to escape my insular world so I decided to simply jump in at the deep end. I quit my safe job of the last 17 years, rented my house out, and bought a ticket back to Asia. This time, though, it was to be a one-way trip.

I certainly had plenty of negative advice of the merits (and sanity) of a 40-something man heading off to seek new beginnings. This was surely something that only youngsters did, according to all the sensible advice I was unwillingly receiving. However, none of that mattered to me, so off I went.

At the beginning I really had no idea where to go; I just knew that I had to go somewhere. The original plan was to travel for a year (I had the funds for that if I was careful), unfettered by any preconceived plans. I just wanted to meet people, experience new places and let each day lead me where it might. A very fluid existence, and all the better for that.

I spent the first six months off the beaten track in both Nepal and India, experiencing great natural beauty alongside scarred landscapes; seeing ostentatious wealth rubbing shoulders with the most abject poverty. The more I travelled and the more interesting people I met, the more convinced I became that a life a little less ordinary was the one for me. I would continue backpacking through Asia for another six months and then get serious about finding a way to earn a living in a different part of the world.

My plans though, were thrown into disarray one hot and steamy New Year's Eve in Kerala, Southern India. My sister managed to get in touch and the news wasn't good. She told me that our mother had been diagnosed with full blown leukemia and I had better get home fast. After a frantic planes, trains and automobiles scenario I was at least able to get home in time to sit by her side, tell her that I loved her and be there with her when she finally escaped from her world of pain.

The period of reflection and the grieving process after Mum's death had me wondering if I was really doing the right thing. Should I not just simply come home, go back to work and be happy to be surrounded by lifelong friends and caring family members? It wasn't long before I decided that the answer to that question was definitely no. You have to be true to yourself. For me, my love affair with travel had only just really begun and I had hardly scratched the surface; the desire to work abroad was as yet unfulfilled, and there were other aspirations I hadn't even started to realize.

My return to Australia following Mum's death was eight years ago. The decision to stay the course and embark on an expatriate life meant a few months of sleeping on friends' sofas and relying on their good will. Then one day a random email to the United Arab Emirates came bouncing back with the good news that I had at last found a job abroad.

For the past seven years I have lived and worked in Al Ain, a traditional Bedouin oasis town located on the border with Oman, though now a bustling small city of 500,000 people. It's a far cry from my hometown and I find myself living and working in an environment where the cultural attitudes, ways of doing things, religion and most aspects of daily life are very different from back home in small-town Australia. Yet, it's a place with a very high expatriate population—a population as culturally diverse as any on the planet, and it's a place where even this small-town Australian feels comfortable and at home. I'm sure the "twenties" me would be quite surprised.

My life in the Middle East is nothing like the expatriate experiences of my friends in Asia, but it is challenging in many different ways and certainly suits me—at least for the moment, until the feet start to get itchy again. I love the fact that virtually every social occasion is filled with people from all over the world, and as a travel-o-holic some of the world's greatest destinations are only a short flight away. Though more change is, as ever, on the horizon, I will certainly never regret or forget my years here in the desert.

I often find that I get asked if I have any regrets (usually straight after "Why are you not married?"). And, it's good question, I suppose. I would have to say, especially in relation to The20Project, that my major regret is not getting a university degree when I was younger. The simple reason for that was that I didn't really find anything at university that particularly interested me at the time. However, the passage of time has shown me that while it is not essential to have a degree to have a successful and happy life, it certainly buys you a whole lot more options along the way. I guess it's never too late to get a degree, as some of my friends have done later in life. I have friends here in the UAE who married at 19, had kids, divorced and ended up getting a doctorate on the wrong side of 50 in a country half way around the world. So, it's never too late; however, lately my journey has been going in a different direction.

Despite that, I've done well enough to find a good job that provides a very decent lifestyle in an interesting and diverse place. Admittedly, when you meet interesting and attractive women, explaining that you work in irrigation rarely sends them into a frenzy of uncontrollable desire. Perhaps I should learn to play the guitar or learn to speak Italian.

So, where does it go from here? By this stage (if you are still reading) most 50-something-year-olds would be telling their stories and dispensing advice to readers from a position of wisdom, security and solidarity. Nothing wrong with that, but it's just not the case with me. Rather, I feel I'm also just at the beginning of something. It is time once again to throw off the shackles, discard the security blanket and leave that safe world behind me.

I have always had a strong interest in the world of film photography and the emotion created by, and captured in, an image, but it had never occurred to me to pursue it professionally. It took a trip to Tanzania in 2009 for me to discover the art of digital photography, and my world hasn't been the same since. After many years, many interests, and a lot of travel I have finally found the all-consuming passion I had been looking for (without even realizing that I was looking for anything at all). I eventually bought my first digital SLR camera and have never looked back, discovering not only a passion for photography but that I was actually quite good at it as well. It has since influenced my travel decisions, given more meaning to solo travel experiences, and given me a lot of satisfaction besides. Combining a love of travel, an interest in the natural world, and an addiction to diving, photography just seemed like such a natural fit.

As I write this, plans are underway to follow through and I aim to reach a professional standard as a photographer. My intention is to take about 12 to 18 months away from the rigid confines of employment and immerse myself in becoming a professional-level photographer. I have yet to decide which genre of photography to specialize in, but portraiture and travel are high on the list.

Perhaps I can make a living from it one day; perhaps not. That said, I desperately need to have at least one period of my life devoted just to myself and my dreams, and not to the dreams and needs of others. If I do need to return to regular employment in the future, I will at least know how it feels to wake up every day and know the absolute freedom that comes with deciding what it is that I want to achieve that day. I realize that taking a leap into the unknown yet again is scary; but not taking the plunge and living with the regret is even more frightening. So, the clock is ticking.

It was not my intention, when asked to contribute to The20Project, to detail a sure-fire path to success and happiness for someone in their twenties. My history is not a conventional one and it's simply one personal journey—all that I have to offer. To be honest, there's not a lot that I regret and I have a lot more to look forward to. The most important thing is to find happiness and a measure of contentment in whatever it is that you do. It doesn't really matter where or how you find it: in work, business, love, family life, art, travel, writing, education and academia, or the accumulation of personal wealth. Whatever it is you want to do, give it all you have got, learn from your mistakes, and never give up. If you are like me then it may not be obvious; but if you keep looking, you will eventually find it. Some lucky folks seem to stumble onto the right path early in life and never look back. I've always been envious and never that lucky.

Of course life throws you many curve balls and constantly changes. But embracing change is positive. We never know for sure where we will end, but just about anything is possible if you commit yourself to it and give it your best shot.

FLAVIO

At 27, Brazilian Flavio Kenup became a world record holder for the longest trip on two wheels. In 2007, Flavio departed from his hometown of Teresopolis in Rio De Janeiro, Brazil and made his way to Alaska on his Traxx Sky 110 motor scooter. He crossed 14 countries and covered over 57,000 kilometers of land during a nine-month period. The Brazilian adventurer discusses some challenges while planning and undertaking this historic trip. This is his story.

1. What inspired you to do this record-breaking trip?

I wanted to learn about the world and found that a moped allowed me to take everything in more than other modes of transportation. Since you are limited on speed, you have to take in the world a little at a time. I was able to stop every day and have good experiences with the people of the towns and cities I visited.

2. How did you get the idea for this trip and how did you start planning it?

After my first trip [on a similar bike, covering 15,000 kilometers in 45 days] to Patagonia in 2005, I got the idea to go to Alaska. Patagonia was a challenge because of the weather and because of the terrain. Being able to take on such a difficult and deserted place gave me the idea of taking on a similar challenge on a larger scale.

Alaska was the ultimate challenge for me, both physically and mentally. I started to plan ten months before I began my trip.

3. Was there something you were looking for or trying to discover as you were doing this trip?

I wanted to learn about different people and countries. I wanted more to travel and to see different cultures. After traveling on a scooter in Brazil and in the countries close by, I grew curious about the countries and cultures further away. I was surprised at how different people can be within one country, like in my country of Brazil, so I wanted to experience the cultures of places different from what I already knew.

4. Was there anything you were trying to get a break from while doing this trip?

No. I just wanted to learn more about everything. I wanted to see what challenges existed while traveling by moped. I had read a lot about people who traveled similar distances but on other types of transportation; the moped was one that I didn't see a lot on, so I wanted to see for myself what it would be like.

5. You did this when you were 27. Was this trip something you felt you could only do in your twenties? Why did you decide to plan this trip at this time?

I decided to do it at that time because it was after my first trip to Patagonia; I didn't do this trip because it was my twenties—I just felt it was the right time for me. I could have done this at 19, in my thirties, or in my forties; I saw many people doing similar trips at different ages and in different categories, like cars, bicycles etc. It just happened in my twenties.

6. Were these other travelers in different categories an inspiration to you?

Some were. I read a lot about people's adventures in different countries and I grew curious of what it would be like to experience this type of challenge for myself. I had a dream that included Alaska; for other people their dreams included different places. Some people just traveled to travel, without one final destination in mind. For some people who travel for years at a time, my short trip was nothing out of the ordinary. This made me hopeful that my goal of reaching Alaska would be possible.

7. Many would worry about how their families would respond to such a huge change. How did your own family react?

They didn't like it because they worried so much. At the time I decided to do the trip, none of my family had ever been outside of Brazil so this trip [which was mostly outside Brazil] made them worry. People had heard about some of the conflicts happening in different places like in Colombia and they were concerned about my safety. When you know the world only through the daily news and when the daily news tells you only about people doing bad things to each other, it makes the world seem like an unsafe place. The thought of me crossing some of the corrupt people you hear so much about was a scary thought for my family. Ironically, Colombia was one of my favorite countries; I always felt safe. I had never before come across such kind and beautiful people.

Mostly though, they worried that the motorcycle wouldn't be strong enough to complete the trip. They didn't know anyone who had traveled in this way [alone and for such a long time] and hadn't heard about something similar being attempted, so they feared that my goal would not happen on this type of transportation. After the third month of my trip, they believed more in the motorcycle. The good thing, though, was that as soon as I began the trip, they then believed in me. It was the moped that they doubted more.

8. What were some challenges you had in planning this trip?

Part of the planning included seeing about visas and other permits; sometimes that got complicated. Within and between countries, a big worry for me was the conflicts in countries like Chile, Ecuador, Colombia and Venezuela. In Bolivia, there were political conflicts weekly. Another challenge—probably the biggest for me—was not being able to reach Alaska in time. I had a time to be there and a time to leave. My goal was to be there before August 15th. After this time the roads would get icy and if they closed, that was the end of my trip. There was no getting to the Arctic Circle at this point, so I had to plan carefully around this, otherwise I wouldn't have been able to reach Alaska.

9. What was the most difficult thing for you to leave behind as you undertook this trip? Was it somebody or something?

My routine life: my normal life like my job and the gym where I would train. Jiu-Jitsu has been part of my life for the last 25 years, so seven years ago when this trip occurred, being without others to practice the sport made me a little bit nervous. Even though it wasn't the same, I committed to daily exercises that included Jiu-Jitsu.

Leaving my friends behind was also difficult—the most difficult, in fact. I lived in a small city where most people know each other very personally, so my friends were more than people I would see once in a while; they were like family. For ten months before, I decided to prepare myself to be alone because that was going to be the most difficult part about traveling. I would practice for my nine-month journey to Alaska by taking trips to some nearby parks or mountains by myself for a few days at a time. I knew on my trip there would be parts where there wouldn't be phones and I wouldn't be able to have contact at all with other people. It's hard to leave your routine because it gives you a sense of security and having people near you who will always support you is so easy.

10. What would your advice be for people who face negativity when trying to undertake something similar?

Just plan what you want to do and make it happen. I couldn't have done this if I didn't plan at least five months ahead. When you start to plan, it's like you've already started the trip. If you don't make a plan, it's only a dream and you're likely to forget it in a few days. As soon as you start to plan and study about a place, you start to see the problems you may have and then you become prepared and you believe that you can do it. A trip like this sounds difficult and seems to many impossible, but once you commit yourself, it can happen.

11. You completed this trip without carrying any type of technology to contact others (no electronic devices like computers or cell phones). How did you find your life to be without daily access to these luxuries?

It wasn't hard. Mostly, I would use Internet cafés to send emails and update my website so people could keep up with me along my trip. Sometimes I would use the computers of friends I met along the way. Sometimes (one or two times a month) I would call home.

12. What would you say to people who feel like they need to be constantly connected to others by cell phone or computer, since you felt you could live your life for an extended period of time without such things?

If you have a life that involves work, school, or a kind of job where you have many responsibilities, for sure you need a phone to keep up with what you're doing. I think people don't need a cell phone for a trip though, especially one like this. If you have some sort of problem on the road, the people you contact may not understand what you're doing and may encourage you to give up and at that instant you may want to do so. Afterwards, you'll realize you made a bad choice. That's why I chose, and I advise others, not to take a cell phone. Sometimes it's handy, but most of the time when you miss people and you call them, they'll miss you and they'll want you home. They'll tell you what you want to hear at the moments you doubt yourself and then it's easy to turn back.

13. How has your life changed after doing this trip?

Many great things happened for me after this trip. The greatest change that occurred was really unexpected; after my nine months going through other counties, I gained confidence in other areas of my life. Before this trip, I was unsure of the direction my life was headed. I mean, I had my routine in Brazil and I could have kept that for a while longer, but eventually there would be a day where I would realize that what I was doing was not fulfilling. After my trip, the sky was the limit for me personally and professionally. When you are faced with a broken-down bike in remote parts of the world with bad weather and you can only get help from people who may not understand you right away, you have no choice but to get through it. Nothing that I could face professionally, I felt, would be that tough—everything seemed doable. I believed in myself to have enough patience and confidence to do what I set my mind to.

I decided that I would practice Jiu-Jitsu in the US with a friend of mine and see what opportunities I could find there. In the US, I got the idea to open up a Jiu-Jitsu academy in Florida. I returned to Brazil to make a plan for my gym, and then took a job in Abu Dhabi, where I would save up enough money for this next dream. Abu Dhabi was a great opportunity because it challenged me to learn a new language (English, incidentally) and to live in a country where the culture was so different from mine. In Abu Dhabi I had to teach students in the public schools, and because it was the start of something new in the UAE, it made me happy that I was helping to create something different.

I eventually opened up a gym in Florida like I had planned, but after a few years of being there I decided to return to Abu Dhabi where I felt that I had more opportunities. I feel many people would settle with something that they had dedicated so much time to because that's what you do; but I know that there is nothing worse than to make a bad move just because it's easy. I am happy to be in Abu Dhabi where I now play a greater part in the Jiu-Jitsu school reform. The first time I had worked here, there were 40 Jiu-Jitsu instructors in the schools, and now the program has grown so much that there are about 160 coaches. I am proud to be part of something great, and I am happy that this sport has helped make so many lives better.

If it hadn't been for my trip, I would have not had the idea to do so many things. When you wake up one morning and are faced with a herd of moose outside of your tent in the wilds of Alaska, you survive. But as much as people say that life is hard and is all about surviving, nothing (to me) is as hard. The hardest obstacles are the ones you create for yourself in your mind.

HEATHER

THE EARLY YEARS

I was a good student, but not a great student. I did make it onto the honor roll most years, but will never forget the semester I was given an F in algebra—that class still haunts me today. In fact, I'm one math (algebra) class away from my associate's degree, but at the age of 43 the thought of going back to school is extremely unappealing. I think I could have been a great student if I had done less socializing and more studying. Nevertheless, looking back I think that, for me, the socializing was a good thing. I've always been a social person and it has helped me to be the person I am today.

At age 11 I "knew" I'd own a business one day. I wasn't sure what kind of business, but I knew I wanted to own one and do my own thing. Around that same time I took over a paper route in the condo complex where we lived and used that opportunity to create my own business cards using index cards as a means of letting my customers know that I was also available to babysit for their children. This was the beginning of my drive toward reaching my goal.

Jumping into entrepreneurship at 11 wasn't the grand thing I thought it would be. It turns out I'm not a big fan of small children; so, babysitting probably wasn't the direction I should have gone. However, during some of those long nights of babysitting I had time to dream and think of what my life would be like in the future as a business owner. It was about this time I decided I wanted to own a bank and I picked out a name for it—Stafford-Lewis Banking Association. A bank, you ask? Well, why not a bank? It took me a few years to realize you don't just decide to own a bank. I'll admit, though, that I still dream of this today.

I continued my paper route for a couple of years, until my family moved from Connecticut to South Carolina. While in South Carolina I was hired for my first "real" job at just shy of 15 years old. I started small and worked for a family-owned department store putting labels on mailings being sent to customers about upcoming events in the cosmetics department. Then I became the youngest employee to work as an elevator operator, and after that was promoted to working the customer service department. I learned a lot of very important lessons in those early years. The most important: a good attitude and hard work do pay off. I was able to buy and do things friends my age couldn't, and I was able to start a resume before I was 16.

Life lesson #1: You are never too young to start planning your life—and it's okay to be the youngest person on the job. (One day you will be the oldest person on the job.)

WORKING MY WAY THROUGH HIGH SCHOOL

Once I started working, I never stopped; I'm not sure I know how to not work. I come from a family line of hard workers, and the belief that you have to work for anything you want. We moved back to Connecticut before my junior year of high school, and not long afterwards I heard that our town hall office was looking for someone to work after school on a project putting old files on microfiche (yes, I'm THAT old). *As you read this are you heading over to Google to find out what microfiche is?*

After I started working at the town hall, I also took another job at a local retail store working in the women's department. At the age of 17 I was going to school all week, working after school at the town hall for two hours and then heading over to the retail store (D&L) to work from 5:00–9:00 p.m. two to three days a week and weekends. I continued to work two jobs until around age 28 because I was so used to doing it and didn't know how to deal with downtime.

I met people at those jobs that I stayed in touch with for many years, some still today. At D&L I was trusted to run our customer service desk some nights, which meant I was in charge of the cash vault on those shifts—a job not usually given to someone so young. I was quite proud of myself, and it lead to a higher-paying job at Filene's a couple years later. I stayed at Filene's for seven to eight years working nights, weekends, and any and all school breaks. I knew I would not be heading to college right after high school, so it was great to have a good job.

Life lesson #2: Your first job(s) can help you form amazing relationships with people you may keep in your life for a long time. Work hard, pay attention, be polite and honest because you never know when you might need to lean on one of those people for help.

HIGH SCHOOL IS OVER...NOW WHAT?

When I graduated, my first full-time "I've-graduated-from-high-school" job was at a company called Electric Boat. They build submarines for the U.S. Navy, and since both my father and stepfather were in the Navy it was an intriguing place to me. This job only lasted about three months because it was a male-dominated place at the time. Being an independent, aggressive woman (read that as "doesn't like to be told women should stay home and cook") I decided I should find a place where I could be myself. As with any job I've had over the years, I still learned quite a bit in those three short months. I learned how to bite my tongue when necessary, how to work with men (which today I prefer), and how to hold my head up and stand up for myself when needed.

I moved on from Electric Boat to a car dealership, and spent the next eight years working for various car dealerships in the area. That first dealership taught me lessons that would prove very helpful when I owned my own business. I will never forget the days of working at that dealership and watching them experience financial problems and spending hours waiting to find out if it would be safe to cash my paycheck. Little did I know that experience would come in handy so many years later!

The years in the automotive business introduced me to people I am still proud to call friends. And working my way up from cashier to assistant office manager through the years helped me learn so many different office techniques, accounting principles, and other customer service-related things important to know when you decide to own and operate a business. I learned how to do accounts receivable and payable, payroll, time tracking and much more. All of these things were feeding my love of wanting to run my own business one day.

While working at one of the dealerships I took a part-time job at a salon and was taught how to give manicures and do acrylic nails. This is where it really "clicked" for me. I was a nail technician for a couple of years, was promoted to a part-time receptionist position and eventually to salon manager. Managing the salon was one of my favorite jobs. For a short time I also worked at a well-known salon and resort spa in Connecticut. That's when I realized that I wanted to eventually own a salon and spa.

In March 1998, when I was in my late twenties, I decided to move to Georgia where my mother and stepfather were living. They had told me many times that the opportunities there were much greater than in Connecticut, so in less than two weeks I sold almost all of my belongings, got in the car at 5:00 p.m. on a Friday, arrived in Georgia at my parent's house Saturday night, interviewed for a job on the Monday, started working on Wednesday and didn't look back!

My first job in Georgia was at a small aerospace hardware company owned by three brothers. It gave me another taste of working in a small family-owned business and got me thinking even more about having a business of my own. I taught myself the fundamentals of using AutoCAD and drew a three-dimensional bolt, learned how to write a standard operating procedure manual, took a class to become an ISO2001 auditor, and much more.

During this time I decided to go back to school and attempted to work toward a college degree. My first love had been accounting, but I soon realized it wasn't really what I wanted to do. I received a certificate in human resources management and another in organizational leadership.

While in school I did a case study and presentation to the business department head suggesting that a small group of students register for a course that was listed, but unavailable, and write the curriculum for it with him during the semester, earning credit while doing so. We successfully completed the task, and the next year the course was offered to other students. This was a true test in how to work with others to accomplish a common goal (and a test of patience for me as I'm a "just going to do it myself" kind of girl).

Life lesson #3: You are going to work with people you don't like. Get over it and be the better person, and learn to work as a team.

MY LATE TWENTIES, THIRTIES AND BEYOND

I welcomed my thirties with an attitude of "I can do anything" and the thought that somehow I would figure out how to own a business. I even went so far as to set up a new email address: trynewthings@xxxxx.com. In hindsight, the email address was probably not a good idea because I was also on a dating site at the time, and it gave a false sense of hope to some guys, I'm sure!

I did some traveling, worked a lot and ran my first marathon in Negril, Jamaica (to raise money for the American Stroke Association). I mean, if you are going to accomplish something you never in your life thought you would (I never even participated in sports in school) it might as well be in Jamaica, right?

The whole time I've been in Georgia I've lived with my mother and stepfather. I moved here with every intention of being with them a year (they would probably laugh at you if you asked them about it) and moving onto bigger and better things and a cute little house somewhere. The truth is that living with them has been great for all of us. My stepfather used to travel a lot and has worked strange hours on and off for years, so rather than my mom being home alone and me being in another home alone we can be there for each other. I can watch the house and pets if they go somewhere and vice versa. The fact that we get along better than most parents and kids is a huge deal. My mother and I have been great friends my whole life.

Nine years ago my stepfather took a new job that was quite far from our house; my mother and I were already traveling through horrible traffic to our jobs, so the decision was made to move closer to our jobs. Living with them proved to be a saving grace, and proof that God is always one step ahead of us. Within the first year of living in the new house we visited a church in the area and on that first visit I met a woman who was interested in selling her salon and day spa. This was the start of what was to be my dream come true.

I spent a year and a half working with a counsellor at the Small Business Development Center to put together a business plan and a financial plan to get funding to buy the salon. I left no page unturned, and with my parents' help I set out on the adventure of a lifetime. In September 2006, we signed on the dotted line and I became the proud owner of my own business.

I made mistakes in my journey to business ownership—many, many mistakes. I didn't trust my instincts, I listened to others, made too many changes too soon, bit off more than I could chew and then some. I also discovered some things that had been done in the past didn't work with my personal beliefs in how a business should be run and it hindered me in ways I didn't expect.

Just shy of two years into owning the business, the economy started to take a turn for the worse. Houses being built around the area were left unfinished, as were strip malls and other buildings. Stores were closing and I was running out of time and money.

April 24, 2014 is the six-year anniversary of closing my business and losing the dream I thought I had worked my whole life to accomplish. People say that the memory of something sad/bad that happens to you dulls as time goes by, but I honestly miss the business as much, if not more, today as I did the day it closed. However, I am no longer conflicted by it, and no longer cry over it or feel like it's the worst thing that ever happened to me. I can look back on it and see the many lessons in it.

If it weren't for my parents, my friends and my faith I would not be where I am today. All of these things contribute to my ability to see things for what they are—a learning experience. Sometimes, while going through something negative we feel like there is no way we will survive or be able to learn from it; but the truth is, every single thing we do teaches us something.

As you move through life, ask yourself what you can learn from it. If you can't find a lesson in it, look just a little bit deeper. The lesson is there. Keep a journal, look back and reflect on it so that you are always learning. Never, ever stop learning.

Because of my tenacity, I am back to working fulltime in corporate America and just celebrated my fifth year as an employee, after spending a year as a contractor. In addition to this, I also started helping a friend sell her amazing products at the local farmer's market. Because of Heather and her awesome business—Rinse Bath & Body—I was able to earn extra money and remain as close to being an entrepreneur as I could without actually owning the business. She let me have free rein to do shows and events, and manage everything as if it were my own.

I decided to make myself an apron to wear at the market and that became the start of my new business and blog—GeminiRed Creations. I started sewing and making other handmade items. I first launched my business on Facebook and Etsy and eventually started my own website. My friend Kristen of K.Leigh Creative designed my website and catapulted me into cyberspace and now I'm doing custom orders and enjoy my time as a business owner again. No, it's not as grand as I had planned, and it's not a big business that I can do fulltime and make enough money to pay the bills, but it's MY business and I love it!

Life lesson #4: When one dream ends in the way you didn't expect, just pick a new dream, new path, or new passion. It doesn't have to be the end of your life as a dreamer!

Learning how to do my own accounting, handle customers, handle complaints, work with vendors and everything else over the years has brought me this far. One day I hope to own a small gift shop co-op where I can sell my wares and have other small businesses share their items with my customers as well. In this shop I also want to sell fabric and have a space in the back for sewing on site and teaching classes. It will happen—I have faith in myself, and I know others do, too.

I dedicate this to my parents, Donna and Daniel Lewis, who stood by me as I set out to buy the salon and who give me a roof over my head while I continue to pay back the SBA loan for my closed business, as well as my dad and stepmom, Calvin and Susan Stafford, who have also believed in me throughout my journey.

Life lesson #5: Your parents are not the enemy. Even when you think you "hate" them for one reason or another, they are the

people who will pick you up, dust you off, and send you back into the game!

I will leave you with my favorite quote from Winston Churchill. I sign all my emails with this and think of it often.

"NEVER, NEVER, NEVER GIVE UP."

HILARY

Let's start with a few numbers…

- I have traveled to 41 countries (adding 3 more to the list this year),
- lived in 7 of them (for over 6 months),
- completed 5 various post-secondary degrees (and starting my PhD in 2015),
- have logged well over 1,500 scuba dives,
- belong to 3 different professional organizations,
- have a secondary business as a photographer (and maybe a third as an author),
- and have no pets, no plants and no kids.

A few people have suggested that I am a bit of an overachiever. I prefer to think of myself as a problem solver and an explorer. As I write this chapter for The20Project, I am in the middle of my 35th year, but some days I don't feel over the age of 16, let alone a functioning adult with a plan!

IN THE BEGINNING

I grew up in a suburb outside of Toronto, Canada in one of those middle-class movie-esque type neighbourhoods complete with a cul-de-sac and a pool. My parents both worked and I was a latch-key kid of the eighties. For the most part, I had a fairly typical childhood. I tried every sport/activity under the sun—of course I couldn't decide on one; and, while I was never really a remarkable student, I definitely always had the thirst for adventure and was never really satisfied with the status quo.

Those who know me would not be surprised to also find out that I grew up on a street full of boys and more than once was scolded by my mother for playing in the dirt and coming back to the house covered from head to toe in mud (in the dress my mother made me wear, of course!). Following my big brother around caused more than one sibling fight, and in the evenings we were called home by my father's whistle as the street lights came on in the neighbourhood. Pretty normal stuff, right?

Between my childhood and university there is probably an entire book's worth to write about, but I will save that for another time. Suffice to say, I ended up at an all-girl's boarding school in Toronto for three years and discovered a love for rowing. This landed me at the University of Western Ontario at 17 (one year early) where I spent two years floundering. My life revolved around getting up at 4:00 a.m. to be at the boathouse for the early morning briefing; then sleeping through classes during the day because I was exhausted, and working out again in the afternoon. I made it through the first year with a little concentrated effort at the end to get passing grades, but in my second year there I was definitely not doing well. I was following the "normal" path and yet had no direction, but thought I should go into political science or maybe law… All I knew at this point was that I was failing to thrive and I really needed to figure out what to do with my life.

So I did what any other rational 'lost' person would do and signed up for a gap year on a Student Work Abroad Program!

I remember the scene when my parents dropped me off at the airport for the very first time and very first flight by myself. I was heading to Australia on a one-year working visa and it was really hard to say goodbye. Everyone was crying, but I remember feeling this budding excitement, like butterflies in my stomach; and it was this feeling that carried my feet forward and into the unknown.

Landing in a new country where you have never been, there are times that are lonely and all you want to do is throw in the towel and go home. But, one thing that I have learned is to stick with it and find the place you are meant to be, or the people you are meant to be with.

When I landed in Sydney after my first Pacific crossing I didn't know which way was up. Thank goodness the program had arranged for a hostel for the first few nights, and consequently I ended up spending the first few weeks in town with the other kids in the program. After a while I started to get antsy and headed out on my own; I moved clear across town to another suburb and joined a rowing club. A few days later I was on a payphone in tears to my mother—I was lonely. I didn't have any friends, no job and just didn't feel like I fit in. My mother said the best thing to me during that conversation that has stayed with me to this day—"*You can always come home.*" Simply, she was saying that she supported me through whatever, and in the end it was my decision, but my parents would always be there for me.

I am fortunate to have parents that support me like this, and I think this gave me the courage to take risks and explore even further than I would have otherwise.

So, after that conversation, I evaluated my options and decided to pack everything up again and move downtown into a central hostel. Here, I had a frame of reference—other people my age from all over the world taking time to explore. So I got comfortable, found a job at a local restaurant as a bartender and moved in with a group of other people from that hostel to a house located just south of the central business district. I had found my tribe.

When you live with backpackers, you tend to meet a lot of great personalities. The other thing that happens is that you become more open to things that you never thought to even take on. I remember sitting in the hostel one day and, although I can't even remember her name, one of the girls asked if anyone else wanted to do their Open Water Scuba Certification. As my dad and brother had recently done theirs, I thought, why not? Little did I know that this experience would have a major impact on my life. At the time, I was content to just finish off my advanced certification course and add both of these to my list of certifications.

This initial trip to Australia taught me a lot about myself and what I am capable of; it also instilled in me a wanderlust that I have yet to lose. Over the years I have met some of my closest friends on my travels. Sometimes I don't see them for years at a time, but I know that when I do it will be like we saw each other yesterday.

OFF THE DEEP END

Although traveling the world was awesome, I needed to figure out what I wanted to do for a career. I knew this was what I had to do because my parents always harped on about this particular point every time I called home!

Since I started my working career as a teenager at summer camps, I thought that taking outdoor recreation would be a good place to start—seeing as I was also a certified rowing coach, ski instructor and lifeguard, not to mention all of the sports from rock climbing to swimming that I took part in. Maybe this would be the right fit.

After two years and a season in Whistler, I ended up working on the Sunshine Coast for a scuba company for the summer; after all, I was an advanced diver from my time in Australia.

This over confidence landed me in the cold waters of the Pacific Northwest. I clearly remember my first dive in cold water; I was in a 7mm wetsuit and freezing cold about 20 minutes into the dive. I don't think I noticed a single thing underwater I was so wrapped up in dealing with all of the gear and buoyancy issues. After getting squared away with the right gear and a few more courses, the only way I can describe that summer was magical. I was diving every other day with a group of people around my age and ended up completing my PADI Divemaster and then instructor's certification.

Being a newly minted instructor with all of the world's possibilities is a heady thing. I decided to stretch my legs again and headed to Bermuda for my first season abroad working in the dive industry. Was I ever in for a surprise!

From the outside, the dive industry looks like a picture-perfect postcard with beautiful people running around in bikinis and floating through the water, teaching perfect students in crystal clear water. Okay, well some of this is true. Actually, most days start early at the dive shop with the compressor going full force, filling tanks, lugging gear around, repairing gear, picking up guests, dealing with boat logistics and also dealing with anything else that can possibly go wrong. After your morning dives, there is usually a lunch dive booked and then two afternoon discover scuba dives; and if you are (un)lucky, someone also wants to do a night dive. If no night dive is booked, you fill your evenings running around filling tanks, repairing gear, ordering new equipment, etc. In addition, if you have some business skills, sometimes you end up doing the end-of-day bookkeeping as well as marketing tasks. To say the least, days off are generally spent doing laundry, staying in air conditioning and avoiding the sand and sea at all costs!

The scuba lifestyle differs from country to country, but there is something about being underwater that always draws me back. I worked exclusively in the dive industry until 2006, taking jobs in New Zealand, the Caribbean, Cyprus, the Philippines and British Columbia.

Looking back on my time in the dive industry, this foundation of running outdoor rec businesses has served me well over the years. It is a dynamic and very fast-paced industry where you find yourself always solving problems and showing a level of leadership far beyond your years. You are responsible for everything from risk management to guest relations.

LIFELONG LEARNING

Although working in the outdoor recreational industry was super fun, I was bored. So in January 2007 I ended up at Royal Roads University starting my MBA. Prior to that I had worked as an independent consultant, but never really felt that I knew what I was doing. So, to business school I went.

When I chose my school I did so because they offered a specialized leadership stream, which was very different from any other program offered at the time. The structure of the program was mainly distance, with three residencies and a thesis (organizational consulting) project. During the second residency, they separated everyone into their streams and the 12 of us who elected to take leadership were put through our paces.

I think the most difficult (and valuable) deliverable of the entire second residency experience was a reflective journal. We really had to dig into how we actually showed up as individual leaders, incorporating everything into this one volume. It included parts of coaching, team building, theory, feedback, and type indicator testing. I will never forget the day during the first week of leadership when my instructor pulled me aside and told me that at the rate I was going, I wouldn't pass. I was absolutely speechless. Up until that point in the course I was coasting. I thought I knew it all and I really wasn't applying myself. Really it was the kick in the pants that I needed to start being more authentic and a better contributor. To say the least, I ended up passing and completed my MBA in December of 2008 and am still in contact with most of my cohort to this day.

If I were to do it over again I would look for a few of these qualities in a master's program:

1. Experienced Classmates. You can't underestimate the ability to share actual working stories to make the content both relevant and timely.
2. Unique focus. Find a subject area that works for what you want to do with your life and not just a generalized class. I think this gets you further in your career and allows you to become more of a subject matter expert in either an industry or service.
3. Modality that works. I have found that as an adult learner I actually do really well as a distance learner, but also need a little bit of face time to re-energize myself (after all, I am an extrovert!).

FINDING PURPOSE

So, what the heck should a scuba instructor, project manager, MBA'er do with her life?

Get into change management of course!

I remember in 2007 thinking to myself that I still had no idea of what I wanted. I did know that I liked the idea of being a management consultant and working for myself, but getting clients was very difficult and knowing the right solutions was even more difficult. During my MBA there was a session on Jim Collins' *Good to Great,* and within the book was his hedgehog concept: "What can we be the best in the world at? (And equally important—what can we not be the best at?) What is the economic denominator that best drives our economic engine (profit or cash flow per "x")? And what are our core people deeply passionate about?"

I think this had the most profound effect on me because it made me think through my skills, experience and come up with a better picture of where I wanted to go with my life, and at the time I chose to start to work towards specializing in organizational development.

After my MBA, a friend with whom I had attended a project management course approached me about a position in the UAE as a project manager at a hospital. So, I packed myself up and spent the next 16 months in a small town in the Emirate of Abu Dhabi called Al Ain.

My time in the Middle East was everything you would expect from an expat life, including all of the great parties, people, activities, travel—and also all of the frustrations. It is a growing experience that I wouldn't trade for anything but I could also write an entire book about my 16 months in the 'sand pit.'

After finishing up in the desert, I spent a few months back in Vancouver figuring out next steps and then another almost four years in large consulting firms (both Accenture and EY) gaining valuable experience and also honing my change management skills. Working in big firms has major up and down sides, but I think it rounded out my education and delivery skills in change management consulting, and it also helped me to identify the things that are important to me in my work/life balance.

I think there are a few things to learn from my story, but a piece of wisdom that I always share with others is to keep building on what you know. I keep my scuba instructor staff rating because one day I will go back to being a simple scuba instructor; but, in the meantime, I keep looking for new business skills that complement what I already know (such as a executive coaching certification or a new photography course).

Definitely always have plan, know where you are going so you are able to ask for specific help along the way. Additionally, play the 'What is the worst thing that could happen' game. This way you keep questioning things and figuring out ways to mitigate any major risks or potential pitfalls.

WHY NOT?

One of the final lessons learned that I want to share with you is the concept of "why not?" I think that on some level I have always been an adventurous person at heart and when I started traveling the world, opportunities came at me fast and furious. At the end of the day, it was always the unexpected ones—where I jumped in with two feet instead of analyzing the opportunity for pitfalls—that have had the most risk, but also the most reward. In December of 2013 I had an email from a friend I had known since high school but really hadn't spoken to for ages. He wanted to know what I was doing in March. Apparently he had an extra ticket to Iceland due to a break-up and needed a friend to travel with. In typical Hilary fashion, I thought about it for an entire 30 seconds and responded with a resounding YES!

The trip was not completely smooth or trouble free, but I did get to go scuba diving between the fabulous stories from the trip; but more than that, these are the things that make life more fun and encourage you to change your perspective on the world.

So, the next time your friend emails you to ask if you want to go to Iceland, your answer really needs to be "Why not?"

EVER AFTER

My journey has been everything but a straight line. I have met wonderful people along the way, I am still supported by my parents/family, I have gained valuable experience and education, and I feel like I am just getting started.

I keep asking questions about what's next. I keep pushing boundaries and trying to figure out what my next step is going to be. I know I will never truly be happy settling for a comfortable existence and I hope that when I am 93 I will still be going out dancing (like my grandfather).

There are still many days that I wake up and can't reconcile the person I am today with the person I was 15 years ago. However, with a big dose of resilience, a tendency for adventure, and a belief that anything is possible I will keep exploring life's challenges.

JUAN

IF YOU'VE MADE IT THIS FAR, YOU ALREADY HAVE AN EDGE OVER YOUR PEERS

I grew up in a typical Latin American family—lower middle-class, family of four boys, and our parents were not educated. My mom's parents believed that only boys go to school, so she never went to school. My dad went to school up until the eighth grade. We didn't come from money. Both my parents worked two jobs just to make ends meet. As kids, we wore hand-me-downs, at times didn't have enough money for lunch, and needed help from the state to purchase necessities. My parents did the best they could to help us out. However, I had to learn (and am still learning) many life lessons through trial and error. And many first-time lessons my parents didn't get to experience! I was a "nobody" hoping to make something of myself.

I started my career as an intern in corporate America. I have worked through the ranks and now work for one of the largest oil companies in the world in Saudi Arabia. I have lived and worked successfully in three different countries, and traveled to 34 countries (and counting). So when the opportunity came up to contribute to The20Project, I told Hilary "count me in!" I feel like I am in a position to offer some advice to 20-year-olds—an age where you are exploring your boundaries, learning new things, and trying to decide what to do, where to go, how to do go about doing it (although it seems as if life is like that all the time).

DO YOU HAVE THAT PIECE OF PAPER THAT SAYS YOU'RE EDUCATED?

Towards the end of my high school years, I didn't have high aspirations. My parents didn't really push us hard to aim high. My goal was to get into a career that required minimal education with maximum payoff. After graduating high school, I worked as a nurse aide, making a little over minimum wage. Working in the medical field was a good starting point for someone with little intention of going back to school, because it exposed me to a professional environment—one filled with educated and intelligent people who motivated me to "think big" and pursue my goals. I also realized that, to get promoted within the organization, I would have to earn a license or a degree.

Qualifications: Must have a bachelor's degree in a related discipline or a master degree (sometimes preferred).

If you haven't already figured it out, you will see the above statement many times over when applying for a job, applying for a promotion, transferring, or joining a professional society. The fact is we live in a world where a piece of paper is proof that you had some level of education and this piece of paper will open many doors for you. Whether your goal is to obtain a certification, a license, or a degree—DO IT! When I began my career, I started as an intern. Three years later, I was making six figures working abroad. Every stepping stone in the company that led up to that point required that I have a degree. There are exceptions, but let's face it, competition is fierce and you need every advantage you can get.

DON'T JUST DO SOMETHING, SET GOALS!

As the New Year approaches, people reflect on what they have accomplished and start to think about their new year's resolutions—or maybe not. Early on in my career, I remember my boss asking me, "Where do you see yourself in two to five years?" I gave him a blank look because honestly, I hadn't thought about it. I just wanted to work and whatever came across my path, I would deal with it then. There is a saying that has always stuck with me: "If you aim at nothing, you will hit it every time." (Zig Ziglar).

Each year I set goals, which some of you may call New Year's resolutions. I think about what I want to accomplish and set at least three realistic goals. One of my hobbies is learning languages. Throughout the process, I set SMART (Specific, Measurable, Attainable, Relevant, and Time-bound) goals. A year and half ago I started learning Russian. I have been to Russia three times. The first time I went (three years ago) I didn't have a clue what people were saying. I'm pretty good at picking up a language fairly quickly, especially if I am immersed in it, so I picked up a few words in my first visit. I told myself that the next time I visited Russia, I wanted to be able to greet people and to ask simple questions about family and friends.

After many Skype lessons, grammar exercises, and reading, I was able to do just that on my second visit. Again, before my third visit, I wanted to speak full sentences and talk about random topics. So, back I went to my Skype lessons, grammar exercises, reading, Russian movie watching, and listening to audio files. Oh, did I mention you have to put in the work to make it happen? I just came from Russia last month (my third visit) and I was able to communicate to Russians about how crazy the weather is, ordering food (especially beer) in restaurants, and talk about my fabulous visit in Chelyabinsk. It's a great feeling when you practice a new language and native speakers understand you. So the lesson is, first set small goals. Realistic goals. Then look where you want to be in three months, six months, one year, five years and so on, eventually completing the bigger goal.

ARE YOU FLEXIBLE?

Whether you realize it or not, it can be very stressful being set in your own ways. The slightest unexpected thing can send you into panic mode. Many of us know someone like this or maybe some of us are this way. Just to let you know, the older we get the more we get set in our own ways, especially if you're single. You don't have to "bend" for anyone. You live alone; maybe have a roommate with whom you don't have to do much compromising. You know how it is.

In your twenties, you get your first "real" job, earning some income, and slowly obtaining more responsibilities. I remember in one of my first jobs, I was always ready to leave at closing time. Work for us ended at 4:00 pm, but sometimes I was heading out the door earlier just to avoid traffic. (Just for the record, at the time I lived in Atlanta with one of the most congested highway systems in the US.) After work, I had a routine—take a nap, go to the gym, eat, and watch my favorite shows. So it was crucial to avoid traffic and save time because that was my routine! So when my colleagues would come to me at the end of the day and give me a task, I would cringe. I wanted to put it off till tomorrow. Talk about not being flexible! Fortunately, I realized this before getting a reputation as not being a team player. This would have hurt my opportunities for any type of advancement within the company.

When I moved to the Middle East, I wasn't sure what to expect, because I didn't do much research into the culture and I just wanted to get out and see the world. Coming from the West, I had a bit of a culture shock. I wasn't able to display public affection (quite a challenge being Latin American!). People didn't understand the concept of personal space. Waiting in a queue in a bank or restaurant, it was common for people to cut in line. People didn't understand English well and I had to repeat myself several times. It was all chaos to me! Needless to say, I didn't do well for the first six months, as I was accustomed to Western life.

When I went back to the states for my first vacation, I was relieved to have left that place. While on my vacation, I had time to reflect. Why had I moved to the Middle East? I wanted to learn about a new culture and travel. When I went back, I was much more relaxed and accepting of my new life in the Middle East. I befriended some locals, giving me the chance to better understand the culture. I was embracing change and felt much more at peace with myself. I have been to more than 30 countries and I can honestly say that I have never been to a country I didn't like.

NEGOTIATING—A SURVIVAL TOOL

The year 2006 was an interesting one for me. I had been in my career for a year and I received a call from corporate asking me if I was interested in a position at the head office. It was unexpected, and I was quite excited. This was an opportunity for me to grow within the organization. After interviewing for the position, I found out that there were several candidates. Somehow, information had leaked out that the other candidates were either too old or didn't have the experience they were looking for. So I felt good that I was the right fit for the job. Within a couple of weeks, I got the offer.

The next step was to negotiate the offer. I knew that in my new position I would get straight salary, unlike my previous position where I was able to earn extra income on top of my base salary with sales and additional service jobs. The first offer was barely more than my current base salary. So how was I going to negotiate? I knew that for me to move, I needed the jump to be worthwhile since I was moving from South Florida to Atlanta. I explained that in my current position, I was getting base pay plus sales. I also mentioned some of the perks I was giving up to take the position in corporate (company vehicle, cell phone allowance, etc.). I felt like I had the advantage—I knew that they wanted a young "buck" who was hungry to learn, and eager to move up and I mentioned that. I focused the negotiating on the end result, how they would benefit by hiring an ambitious employee. In the end, I was able to get

$8,000 more than they originally offered and they ended up with a good employee—at least I thought so!

Negotiating plays a major role in our daily lives, both professional and personal; we negotiate with our family, friends, co-workers, neighbors, and even strangers. In the workplace, for example—anytime you have a great idea and would like to present it to the boss; or you have been tasked to work on a project with a difficult co-worker and you need to discuss roles and responsibilities; or selling and buying a product or service—all require the art of negotiating.

Any time there is a discussion that requires a decision for a particular outcome, negotiating skills are needed—convincing our significant other or spouse (you know you have to be very skilled for this), or settling a dispute with a family member; coming to an agreement with the annoying neighbor; buying big ticket items like furniture, a car, or a home. The list can go on and on.

Negotiating will not only help you earn more money in a job offer, but it will lead you to more of a win-win outcome in settling differences. Whether it is a conflict with a friend, purchasing a home, or settling a credit card bill, negotiating is definitely a much needed skill.

LIFE IS SO MUCH EASIER WITH A PERSONAL COACH

I was brought up in a low middle-class family. My parents were blue-collar workers, both working two jobs to support a family with four kids. As I mentioned, my parents had very little education. So in terms of giving advice, my parents were only able to help us with so much before we had to seek answers elsewhere, sometimes learning things the hard way.

In my professional career, Ron, one of my first, and better, bosses is one reason why I'm where I am today. I guess you can say he took me under his wing when I started in corporate America. Not because he was my boss and I was his subordinate, but it seemed like we had a unique bond, sharing some common interests and engaging in good conversations. I was still wet behind the ears coming into a big company. Ron had been with the company for more than 15 years, so he knew all the ins and outs of the organization. I remember one of my first performance feedback meetings with Ron. He had asked me, "What is it that you want to do in this company? I will do my best to help you achieve it." I thought, wow, how many bosses ask that of their employees. Usually during your performance feedback evaluation, they tell you what you are doing wrong and how you can improve.

Ron had a good network of professionals within the organization, so he knew what department was hiring, who they were looking for, where, etc. At that time, the company had just acquired a franchise in the United Arab Emirates. As I wanted to work abroad and travel the world, Ron approached me and told me about a position the international department was hiring for. Being his mentee, I felt I had an advantage over my peers. In this case, I knew about a job that not so many knew about in the company. He also put in a good word for me, and a reference from Ron within the company carried weight.

Because of my mentor, I was able to score that international position. He also helped me get a couple of promotions within the organization, obtain my professional certification, and get accepted into the master's program that I am currently in. Life has been so much easier with a mentor. Thank you, Ron!

PLAYING WELL WITH OTHERS

I have to admit, I have a bit of road rage. Whenever I get behind the wheel, it's on! No one can cut me off or else I'm going to get ANGRY. And when I'm angry, everyone else pays! Wait—that doesn't sound fair. But that's what used to happen. Long after an encounter took place, I would still be fuming about the guy who cut me off or didn't use his turn signal. I brought toxic emotions home and to work. As a result, anyone on whom I dumped my toxic feelings probably ended up having a worse day.

One of the hardest things in life is actually living with another human being, right? We all have our own ways of doing things, beliefs, thoughts, behaviors, etc. Oftentimes, we get into heated conversations with a loved one, spouse, girlfriend, boyfriend, friend, etc.

I have a twin and although we look alike and have the same interests, we don't think alike. Recently, we had a debate whether to fly our mom business class or economy to the Middle East (from the US). Yeah, it's quite pricey. However, considering our mom is the greatest mom on earth, she deserves to fly with class. But wait, what happens when she gets here? We spent our budget on the airfare flying her business class and we forgot to consider the budget taking her out while she is here for three months! So this debate was going back and forth for a month. Our disagreement was lingering in the back of my mind while I was hanging out with friends, family and even working. So who knows how many people were affected by my toxic feelings from debating with my twin. Needless to say, because of my negotiation skills (grin), I won that one!

In *Social Intelligence and the Biology of Leadership*, Daniel Goleman describes social intelligence as the ability to read others and interact accordingly. In layman's terms, social intelligence is the ability to get along well with others. Learn to transform negative interactions into positive experiences. Yes, I still have road rage, but when the encounter is over I have learned to dump my toxic feelings with it. It took me awhile to make this a habit, but I now feel better about not ruining another person's day by carrying around a negative attitude.

This year, I turn the big 4-0. So far, my experiences and choices have led me to where I want to be in life. I am still working in Saudi Arabia and really enjoying my experience here. I hope that I left you with advice and experiences to prepare for life's twist and turns. When I was 20 I would have loved to have a book like this to read.

JULIA

Twenty is an age of blue-sky possibility. Our early twenties make us old enough to have seemingly limitless freedom and often young enough to have not yet taken on heavy responsibility. Rarely is 20 old enough to have messed things up beyond recovery, and often it is a time that any choice you make can be a formative one. It is exhilarating and tremendously challenging all at once.

I remember thinking I had enough of the big picture figured out at 20 to not have to worry so much about the rest. I was getting educated, and although I had chosen the obscure major of Classical Studies which I hadn't yet figured out how I would use after I completed my degree, I understood I was getting really good at reading, writing and figuring out "why." While my panicked classmates were talking about studying for the LSATs and applying to grad school as we filed into the classroom for our "Classical Greek Sculpture" lecture, I remember smiling to myself, thinking that my newly honed skills of absorbing volumes of information and distilling out the key points would one day come in handy. Little did I know it would become one of my most marketable skills in my post-MBA job hunt.

Though being a lawyer had always been on the table, and was a great thing to tell anyone who asked the question every graduating university student dreads, at 20 I was young enough to not be consumed with what career I would have; I just figured I would have a good one, whatever I ended up doing. I also wasn't worried about buying a house or how I would pay my mortgage. Those seemed like problems for later in life and I was still managing to live in great parts of my city, close enough to work I didn't need my car, but lucky enough to have that little Volvo station wagon to escape to the mountains when I needed to recharge.

In my early twenties I wasn't yet concerned with when I would get married or to whom; though I was really interested in having a boyfriend and not getting anywhere quickly with that. Since the age of 14 I had a clear image in my mind of my perfect mate: he was tall, a country boy at heart who could ride a horse and play guitar. He thrived on the prairies and lived for weekends in the mountains. I had a pretty good hunch I would end up with a cowboy, but in the meantime was just interested in dating a nice camp counselor or a lifeguard.

I made job choices for the love of the work, not for where it might take me, and never for the money. These choices ended up being some of the best I made. I was a camp counselor when my friends were taking on internships they didn't love. While I was lucky enough to have parents who saw value in the leadership skills I was gaining, the friendships I was forming and the fun I was having to help support me through school, I was not beyond worrying sometimes that I was missing out on parties and friendships for never being around in the summers, or for having less spending money during the year. After I graduated from my incredibly practical double major in history and classics, I sold ski vacations to make money to travel Asia and New Zealand.

My first career was firmly in the stretchy pants and yoga lifestyle business. I wasn't making much money but I was figuring out what lit me up, what I didn't want to spend my life doing and, perhaps most important of all, having experiences I would never forget or be able to replicate. Folding black spandex during the slow winter months and restocking racks of brightly coloured tank tops during heat waves may not have been the nine-to-five job that would have kicked off my HR career, but it taught me a lot about running a business where customer service and corporate culture were the only real differentiators. I know this all sounds wonderful and very carefree—it was—but it was also terrifying at times. It was often unnerving feeling like my path was just a little bit different than everyone else's. My youth, wanderlust, and encouraging parents made the world a place full of curiosity and possibility. This shouldn't be a surprise given my favourite poem growing up was Robert Frost's classic, *The Road Not Taken*.

My mum had always told me that my twenties were for figuring out what I didn't want to do. I walked a fine line between embracing that notion, taking on new opportunities with little thought for what would come down the line (always looking for places, roles and relationships that suited my skills and aligned with my passions) and worrying that I was going to mess it all up by not having it all figured out. I had friends who had known since junior high that they would be surgeons or work for NASA. I, too, was passionate about what the future had in store, but at the time none of it aligned to any sort of career path. I am still not sure it does.

I've always loved taking pictures and wandering through towns I've never been to; I love writing and lying in parks and inspiring those around me, but have yet to find a passion that is directly related to a career path.

After the lofty goal of getting into a good university that I had spent my late teens working towards was achieved, I wasn't sure what was next. All the things that people talked about being "big" in life seemed so incredibly far away, and all the things between being too young and being grown up seemed so accessible, so compelling. A house and career, a husband and kids seemed a lifetime away; but world travel, flexible jobs with organizations I adored—whether their products were stretchy pants, ski vacations or summer camps and life skills—and living in any Canadian city were my reality.

So it was in my early twenties that I started to bring things from the realm of "what I didn't know I didn't know" into "what I didn't know," and slowly into the sweet spot of knowing more and more about what lit me up. While working for a resort selling ski vacations, I learned I love casual Tuesday mornings on the slopes, but hate being on the phone with people I don't know. Working at Lululemon taught me that spending Christmas Eve with my family was more important than getting a great discount on hoodies. But it turned out what was supposed to be a short-lived gig selling stretchy pants to pay back travel debt was where I found my groove and started to put my finger on my passion for entrepreneurship and developing people. While law school may have eventually led me to the same conclusions, the route I was lucky enough to take gave me experiences I could never hope to duplicate, and amazing friends in the process. Being open to something I hadn't planned for made me lucky enough to be given a shot at running every part of our small store, from hiring and training our newest educators to managing inventory and learning the finances that went along with it; the late nights cleaning up, the 5:00 a.m. mornings unpacking boxes, and all the yoga classes and great nights out were just a bonus.

It might be surprising that it took me some time to get over the idea that I was not going to be a lawyer. It was something to say when friends, teachers and classmates asked me what was next and I wasn't quite sure of the answer. At times, I promise, this was what I wanted; but more often than not it was a convenient place holder while I discovered more and more about what else was out there, opportunities I hadn't known existed or had been too proud to consider. Eventually, when I talked about being a lawyer the line had changed from an abstract idea to doing something that I could love as well (pursuing a law degree but probably working in business). To be completely transparent, I had no idea what "business" actually meant and I wish someone had told me that doing a law degree to be in business would be a lot less efficient than just getting a business degree.

While I lived my early twenties open to almost any opportunity that felt right and aligned with my passions, I did have a few things figured out. I knew I would always live out west; I hated Toronto (even for having never been there, outside of my airport layovers between school and home). I had grown up with the black prairie soil in the creases of my hands, the cold crisp snow of the Rockies under my skies, and my face and shoulders sun-kissed by west coast summers. To me this was, and still is, heaven on earth and has saturated my soul. The west taught me more about how life works and the wonder of nature than I could ever ask.

Toronto, and everything that came with it was intimidating; it felt tough and cold and grey to me, though I had never stepped foot out of the airport at the time. Having never explored the city, I was unaware of the diverse and robust neighbourhoods, the delicious food, colourful and abundant art and seemingly never-ending line of festivals. I didn't know what I didn't know and had made up something to fill in the gaps. In my mind it didn't matter—I would never end up there anyway.

I always envisioned a lifestyle for myself much like the one I had been raised in, living close to nature and spending as much of my free time there as possible. I would ski on the weekends; my future husband and I would have dogs and drive a station wagon, living near to where I had grown up. Clear in my vision was the desire to be close to my family in distance and in relationships, and to not commute. I would never be a girl who lived in the suburbs. We would have a white wedding in the mountains or near a lake. I knew these things for certain and was unwavering in my decision. While I was enjoying and learning from the opportunities I was taking, I was overlooking many more simply because they did not align with what I thought I knew I knew, and they fell into the what-I-didn't-know-I-didn't-know bucket. One quick word of advice: **don't write something off, whether a career path, a person, a city, or a new bottle of hot sauce, until you've tried it**.

So a few years later, my 14-year-old, pony-riding, camp-going, west coast self would have never seen this coming. Neither would my 20-year-old self, just trying to figure out how to get back out to the prairies and ocean. Even my 25-year-old self, selling stretchy pants and chasing boys at the local pub would have never figured I would end up where I am now.

I have never been to law school. I no longer live out west. I, in fact, live and work in Toronto, and I am with someone who doesn't ski.

I did not end up being a lawyer, but did end up going to business school and it was one of the best things I've ever done. It was one of those flukes of perfect timing, damn hard work and a generous helping of homemade luck. I happened to quit my job by mistake and had just six weeks to relearn high school math, write the GMAT, apply to schools and then cross my fingers and move to Vancouver before anyone could change their minds.

Five years later, I don't sell stretchy pants or teach yoga, but I still work hard at developing and inspiring others in my role at a bank. I don't hesitate to look up when leaving the office—the irony of working at the heart of the financial district is not lost on me. My path here was not direct or typical, but I would be shocked to find someone whose path truly is. Though Toronto was never in my plans, I am grateful I met someone who showed me that it isn't just a city of tall, grey buildings and people who are too busy to smile, but actually a collection of lovely and unique neighbourhoods, easy access to New York—and it is my current home.

It's probably also not hard to guess that I did not end up with a camp boy, or a cowboy. I ended up with someone who doesn't ski and never grew up on the ocean, but who holds me to the high standards I have for myself and helps me meet them. After years of having it never really work out with the boys that seemed right on paper—the ones who skied, who were Calgary born and raised—I ended up falling for my best friend. At the time I wasn't open to a relationship at all; he surprised me with his openness, his undeniable sense of humour and his persistence. Since getting to know him I've travelled more of the world and learned even more about what I didn't know I didn't know. I even love him despite the fact that he cheers for the wrong hockey team.

Looking back on how it's turned out so far, I am grateful that I took the opportunities I did in my early twenties and started to let the pieces of the future I had planned fall away when they no longer served me. It hits me that once in a while that I am nowhere near where I thought I might be when I started thinking about "growing up."

I will always look back on the day I decided not to apply to law school in order to gain more business and people development experience selling stretchy pants. Sitting in the office above the store, my mentor told me of a time in her early twenties when she made a similar choice. Faced with the option to do what she had trained to do her whole life—to sing opera—and to continue on an unorthodox career in the stretchy pants world, she chose the latter. Her advice was that opera, like law school, would always be there and Lululemon may not be. It was pivotal, and while disappointing to a younger version of myself who had her hopes set on long nights in the library and mock trials, it was a decision that led me to business school, the most fun two years of my life and finding my partner, teammate and best friend.

The only thing I wish I had done more of in those years was let go of more along the way, let go of cowboy dreams and my mistrust of anything east of Saskatoon. It can be brutally hard to stop pursuing something you want; but had I known how much I would have discovered, experienced and changed in the last ten years I wouldn't have been so hard on myself for changing the dreams and goals of my 20-year-old self.

Having big goals at every stage of life is not only a crucial part of getting where you want to go, but also of being where you are. They drive us away from stagnation and towards opportunity; the part we sometimes forget is that those opportunities are not always what we planned. It is more than likely life will not unfold exactly as we had imagined. It takes a lot of energy to be constantly working towards something we may have set out in a vision far before we really know ourselves.

I recently learned about leaving white space in my goals and vision boards—a little empty real estate for all those things you never thought could happen because you didn't know better. Since doing this and reflecting on where, at 20, I thought I would be now and where I ended up, leaving part of my future open to the unknown just feels right.

So far, those unpredictable moments have been some of the best. At the end of it, the only thing I wish to leave you with is be open to the things you said you'd never do; be open to what feels right but may not be what you always thought you wanted for yourself. While hard work is a more than admirable trait—necessary, to say the least—often the path of least resistance, no matter how strange, may be the one you actually want to travel. Over the past decade or so I have slowly learned to stop fighting the future a bit. I hope to get better at that going forward. Perhaps that is the advice someone will give me about turning 30.

MARGARET

DO WHAT YOU LOVE.

Pursue the things in life that make you happy, you are passionate about, and everything else will fall into place.

Throughout my life, there were major events that I refer to as turning points that shifted my direction and set me on a new course, but I always pursued the things I loved to do the most. Here is my story.

My parents moved to Canada from Germany in the early 1950s. My father worked very hard as an accountant for a small lumber company. Eventually, he owned his own lumber mill and became a very successful business person in the small town I grew up in, Pembroke, Ontario. My younger brother by four years was to take over the business my father started, as my father was very traditional and believed that only the son should run the business; and for me, he always wished that I get a good education, find a good man and marry.

My father was instrumental in giving me direction, discipline and the courage to venture off into the world without fear. My mother stayed at home to raise my brother and me, so I always had someone to talk to about life's difficulties and joys. My mother is the most loving and gentle person I know. She has the grace and charm equivalent to Jacqueline Kennedy and an air of sophistication, even though she grew up on a farm in Germany with seven brothers and sisters. I remember my mother was always singing around the house and always positive about all aspects of life, and I carry these memories with me today.

Something I learned early on was that I enjoyed my independence and freedom, the ability to decide where I wanted to go and what I wanted to be. I still have a page from my diary that I wrote when I was 14 years old saying, "I want to be free and will only marry later in life. I will work as a secretary for a rich businessman and travel the world." It was the early sixties, after all. I wanted success in my life just like my father, to have a business of my own, and a successful career. My parents were great teachers in giving me direction and giving me so many opportunities when I was young. I am forever grateful to my parents for providing me with figure skating, ballet and skiing lessons, and introducing me to travel throughout Canada, the United States, and Europe.

Growing up, my parents travelled a great deal and always brought home artwork and paintings that filled the walls of our small home. I loved to be creative and was always drawing, working on some arts and crafts project, or designing and sewing my own clothes. The book that most influenced my thinking was Ayn Rand's, *The Fountainhead*. This was partly the reason I loved design and architecture, and my guidance counselor in high school directed me towards interior design. There were only two places in Canada that offered a Bachelor of Applied Arts (Interior Design) degree that I could take: one in Winnipeg and the other in Toronto.

When the time came to go to university, I was so ready to leave the small town of Pembroke with a population of 13,000. I had a steady boyfriend at the time and he wanted to be a lawyer, so he went to York University and I went to Ryerson. Those four years shaped my life considerably.

I was now enjoying my independence and the variety of courses that the program offered was just what I needed. I could take woodworking for the first time (something I could not do in high school, as girls were required to take only the cooking and sewing classes). There were classes in architecture, construction materials, sculpture, drafting, art history, psychology, and graphics. This diversity of subjects was perfect to expand my horizons as this all reinforced what I loved and was passionate about. I also had the opportunity to travel to Scandinavia one summer as part of the school program visiting designers such as Marimekko, Georg Jensen and Alvar Aalto. This trip included Finland, Sweden, Denmark, Holland and Germany. It was a very memorable and powerful trip as it laid the groundwork for my deep love of design and my life choices in what I wanted around me and how I wanted to live.

Interior design led me to working in various companies and gave me all kinds of opportunities. I had decided that commercial design was what I wanted to work in and started designing dental offices as my first job. The opportunity to work with many different clients and spaces was exciting and I loved every moment.

GETTING AN EDUCATION IS THE MOST IMPORTANT THING YOU CAN DO, BECAUSE NO ONE CAN EVER TAKE IT AWAY FROM YOU.

My father always stressed that getting an education would be the most beneficial and rewarding task I could undertake. I believe any education, and not just a formal school program, broadens your opportunities, builds character, and shapes the person you will become. I would strongly recommend a formal education, travel, or just learning about life in general, be curious, and ask questions. Not just the BA, MBA or PhD, but the courses you love most, such as art, carpentry, literature, or gardening, wherever your passion may take you. Try a few things until you find what you love to do the most. If you are not passionate about your work and have the skills that will earn you an income, you will drift and somewhere in the not too distant future hopefully stumble into your dreams.

FOLLOW YOUR HEART; DO THE THINGS THAT KEEP YOU PASSIONATE ABOUT YOUR WORK.

I was always open to new opportunities and was flexible to pursue whatever came to me.

Shortly after I received my degree, in the early eighties my parents bought a convent that was over 6,000 square feet with four acres of land. They wanted to convert it into their residence and offered me the opportunity to design and supervise the renovation work. What an amazing prospect to apply my newly acquired skills to such an intense undertaking. While I was living with my parents I decided to take flying lessons at the local airport. When the house was completed, I also had my private pilot license.

After my parents moved into the house, I headed back to Toronto with a new boyfriend and a great job with the CIBC (Canadian Imperial Bank of Commerce) where I worked with a team to manage the relocation of 1,000 employees from their downtown head office to a new building in the suburbs.

During this work, another great opportunity presented itself when I happened upon a presentation at Ryerson by an alumni student who had gone to York University to complete a master's degree in environmental studies. At the time I was a member of the newly created Facility Management Association in Toronto, which was just starting up in Canada. I went to York University to discuss the possibility of starting the first master's degree in facility management in Canada under the environmental studies department. I spent time in the United States at various universities that already had this program in place, and took courses at York University and Cornell University in Ithaca, New York. This was a very exciting time for me as I developed this program and worked closely with ground-breaking professors, writers, and intellectuals in Canada and the United States.

Sometimes inspiration and direction can come from anywhere. Always be open to taking the opportunity to be innovative, original, and daring.

YOU ARE ONLY GIVEN WHAT YOU CAN HANDLE.

At times when I thought I could not possibly handle a situation or challenge and I was close to giving up, I would remember this saying and have the strength to carry on. Life has not been a smooth ride where everything is in perfect alignment. The choices I have made along the way I do not regret because in each event there was a lesson that created the person I am today. So many times we look back on a decision and wonder if a better or different choice may have led to another ending. No regrets—we can only move forward.

While attending school I became pregnant with my son, Justin, and I decided to raise him on my own. I had no concerns or fears that I could do it all: being a mom, school and work. My son, wrapped tightly in the baby carrier on my chest, came with me to classes and the library. I hired a nanny, and my parents helped whenever I needed to travel and write my final thesis. I am so grateful for their support.

Having this master's degree now opened so many more doors. Ryerson offered me a position teaching facility management courses, which I did for a few years. I had speaking engagements for the Facility Management Association conferences and I travelled to Boston, New York and Dallas. Companies such as IBM, Credit Union Central of Saskatchewan, and Rothmans offered me consulting work. This was the peak of my career; I had my own consulting business, teaching at Ryerson, travelling to various speaking engagements and raising my son.

One memorable moment for me came when I was flying from Toronto to Vancouver on business, and there in the *EnRoute* magazine was an article on my accomplishments in the facility management field.

THE ONLY REAL SECURITY IN LIFE LIES IN ENJOYING LIFE'S INSECURITY.

While Justin was in grade two we discovered that he was having difficulty reading in class and could not comprehend the written word. We had test after test, visited psychologists, and finally the news that he had a learning disability.

Again, I reached a turning point when I realized that I needed to be with my son and help him through his school years. I sold my house in Toronto and moved back to Pembroke, my hometown, to live in a small community with support from my parents to raise Justin.

I threw myself into the area of learning disabilities and read everything I could on the subject. The most challenging aspect was to keep up his self-esteem. I started to educate his teachers that not all kids learn the same, and children with learning disabilities required other stimulation and alternative methods to learn.

I joined the Parents' Association and became a member of the Renfrew County Board of Education – Special Education to raise awareness on the needs of learning disabled children. During this time, I also started the local chapter of the Learning Disabilities Association and held lectures for parents and teachers. Then I went on the speaking circuit to various conferences in Canada and spoke on how each child is different, and teachers need to understand that there are different ways of learning and teaching these special children.

I assisted in the classroom and became a mentor for other children who had not just learning disabilities, but behavioural difficulties. During this time I so enjoyed being a mom. Justin and I travelled often to Mexico, Disneyland and St. Lucia. As well, I took Justin to skiing, karate, horseback riding and swimming lessons, always encouraging his strong skills. I look back now and am thankful that I had those years devoted to raising him. The drive and passion I had during this time to make changes was so rewarding.

To make a living I bought houses, renovated and sold them again. I also bought cottages and developed waterfront properties in the area. The renovation, design, and construction work was stimulating and I enjoyed the creative and physical work, as well as spending time with Justin.

YOU WILL ALWAYS LAND ON YOUR FEET.

Another saying that my father told me often.

I knew that I needed to make a change, and another turning point presented itself when Justin was about to start high school and I needed to get back to work and continue my career. Recognizing that change is necessary is a very valuable instinct. Follow your passion.

During my time with Justin and spending time in Pembroke, I continued to fly, obtained my real estate license, went sailing in the British Virgin Islands where I completed my Learn to Cruise Basic and Intermediate certification, and Justin and I completed a scuba diving course. I also upgraded some of my facility management software skills and then moved to Vancouver to start a consulting job with ICBC (Insurance Company of British Columbia). I had to complete building assessments with the new software tool that I learned. The task was to complete an assessment on all the claim centers and driver services locations in British Columbia. What a wonderful opportunity to see the province.

I found the perfect white house to live in by the ocean in Deep Cove, which was a dream come true. Justin was off to school only a few blocks away and I had a great consulting business for various clients. Through the Facility Management Association I belonged to in Ontario, I was able to find numerous opportunities for consulting work in Vancouver. I became very involved with the BC association as their event manager, bringing in speakers on various topics to inspire and educate the members. This allowed me to meet a number of new contacts and network in the field, thus increasing and expanding my business. I was able to live comfortably in the Cove as Justin finished high school.

One day while walking on the beach I saw a group of people on the water in rowing sculls and knew instantly that this was something I wanted to do. I signed up for lessons and before long I was part of the masters rowing group getting up at 5:00 a.m. to be on the water.

I loved the sport, the peace, and Zen-like feeling of quiet mornings and the rhythm of the boat as it skimmed over the calm water. Over the years, I went to numerous provincial and national regattas and eventually became a coach and then program manager for the Deep Cove Rowing Club. Having a sport like rowing was very grounding and rewarding.

TREAT OTHERS LIKE YOU WOULD WANT TO BE TREATED.

Family is a very important aspect of my life. My mother is my best friend and confidante, and she is always happy, loving, and positive about everything in life. She is my role model on how to be gracious, loving and patient.

My son will always be a constant with his unique ways of seeing the world and his sheer genius with ideas and insights for the future. My father was my mentor on how to run a business and to be good to your clients and vendors, by treating them well and be open and joyful. He was always pleasant and happy with everyone, and enjoyed a good joke and to have laughter around him. I only drew closer to my father near the last few years of his life, where we talked more and shared our lives more than ever before.

Friends throughout life are very special. My first boyfriend when I was in high school is still today a good friend. Even though we do not see each other often, I know I can count on him in a time of need. I also have other friends from high school and university that I keep in touch with, and I cherish sharing life's everyday adventures with my friends.

I have found that friends who are close to your heart's age are so important. In my heart, I still feel so young and adventurous and I want to be around younger groups for inspiration. As I get closer to the so-called retirement age, I do not want to talk about getting old, quitting work and downsizing into care homes. There will be time for that later. Each day is a gift, a reward worth living. Be positive, smile and be thankful each day.

My involvement in church when I was young was also a very powerful influence in my life. I was involved in youth retreats, and my two best friends during high school both married pastors. My Christian upbringing had a big impact on how I relate to others.

I taught Sunday school when my son was young, and I will always remember one Sunday session where I asked the class to write about what they saw themselves doing in the future. One boy wrote he wanted to be a famous country singer, marry and have three kids, and live in Nashville. Today he is living this dream. He lives in Nashville, is married with children, and tours the United States and Canada. He won best new Country video single in 2013. Dreams do come true, so aim high.

Even though religion was a big part of my life in my youth and when my son was young, today I am no longer involved in a traditional religion or church. Once when travelling on business to Vancouver, while I was still living in Toronto, I read the book, *Out on a Limb*, by Shirley MacLaine, which changed my thinking on how I viewed the world. Today I am spiritual and believe in the powers of the universe and the need to visualize what you want in your life.

"Be careful what you wish for," because on a number of occasions the universe has delivered amazing adventures and challenges. In addition, I am very aware of life delivering me the things I need when I need them the most, and not necessarily the things I want.

DO EVERYTHING IN BALANCE—WORK, LOVE, FOOD, PLAY.

Perhaps I overindulged in some of these areas over my lifetime, and it has caused me pain, discomfort, and losing focus on my goals. Goal setting is critical. I have always cut out pictures from magazines of where I want to live, what I want to wear, and how I want to interact with others. I have always searched for calm, patience, and serenity; however, when I am stressed, in pain, or angry I recognize this as something in my life is not in alignment.

Many circumstances have shaped my thoughts, my dreams, and my direction in life, but the underlying values and goals are still there and will always guide me. I have enjoyed trying new adventures—skiing, sailing, scuba diving, rowing, kayaking, Kung Fu, Tai Chi, Qi Gong, art classes, mediation retreats, and yoga—whatever life offers, and each new skill acquired continues to shape and develop who I am today. Never stop trying something new.

There is a binder that I started in my teens and continue to add to, as it carries all my dreams, goals, sayings, pictures of what I see in my life. I like to go through it on occasion to keep myself on track—to alter occasionally—but all the same goals and dreams keep resurfacing. Life is constantly changing and the old traditions and choices may no longer apply. Go with the flow and do not be held back by traditions. In all stages of life, we dream of the future, where we will be, and what we will be one day.

Never pretend to be what you are not. It may be fun at the time, but the consequences can be demoralizing. Be true to yourself; listen to others' advice and stories, but the ultimate decision is yours and yours alone.

I met an 80-year-old woman originally from California on a bus in Mexico once. She made it clear that she still had a job—an artist. She had travelled the world and was now living in Mexico with her boyfriend. She was dynamic, dressed impeccably and had a smile and love in her heart that I will never forget.

I also had a great aunt who lived to be 100 and she played the violin, painted, and lived her life with grace and enthusiasm. I have been keeping her in my thoughts for decades and see myself in the future living as she did.

Find a mentor or person who you can follow and ask for advice. That person will reflect a part of you that you want to strive towards and see yourself as in the future. Use your imagination and shape how people will remember you, what you leave behind, your legacy, and your life.

DO WHAT YOU LOVE.

There are so many choices, so much freedom to do positive and lasting work. Never let life simply pass you by; be passionate, be bold, be brave, be yourself, and most of all enjoy each moment that you are here to do what you love. Ask yourself what makes you happy, what is important to you? Then design your time and life around those items.

MICHELLE

The story of my twenties is an adventurous one, with twists and turns, heartache and worry, fun and disaster, anger and exultation, happiness, joy and more than a few tears. I've learned that while it's never easy to try and make a living out of traveling and working; support can come from the unlikeliest of places, and often it's the experiences we have at home that can be the most useful on the road ahead. The road through my twenties has been interesting, and even though they are over, this crazy adventure I'm on doesn't show any signs of stopping.

I was born in 1984, in North Vancouver, Canada. In elementary school, I used scrunchies that were neon green with black polka dots to hold up my side ponytail. Some very expensive cars had phones—attached to the middle console by a cord of course—and computers were still ten years away; I learned to type on a typewriter, and Zach Morris was the most beautiful boy I had ever seen.

After 13 years of public school and early acceptance into university, I thought that I wanted to be a high school teacher. It just seemed like a good idea—a steady job, with a couple months' vacation in the summer. My parents hadn't gone to university; a post-secondary education wasn't necessary in their day. Fast-forward to my generation and no one would look at you without a degree. Even then, I knew it wasn't the degree that meant so much, but the idea behind it: you could commit to something for four to five years, work through it, and emerge on the other side ready to commit to your career for the rest of your life and work some more. At the age of 18, I was prepared to do this, but by the time I hit 20, after a couple of years of university, I knew the path I was on wasn't the right one for me. I toyed around with a few different ideas, but ultimately decided to finish my degree and see what happened from there.

In the last year of my degree program, I decided to look into doing an exchange semester abroad. Although the deadline was the following morning, I somehow managed to get everything together and was accepted.

To make sure I had enough money to fund my adventures, I took a second job as an office assistant in a construction/development company my parents' friends owned. I learned how filing systems really work (it's not all alphabetical!), how to fill in government forms, perform endless bank reconciliations, and gained an understanding of what life in the "real world" was like. I enjoyed my time playing adult in the office, and have carried the skills I learned there with me around the world and back. All cashed up, in the fall of 2006, I headed off to Scotland for the final semester of my undergrad. It turned out to be one of the best decisions I've ever made and changed my life forever.

I loved the freedom of going to a brand-new place, and the excitement of trying to figure it all out. There was a new currency to identify, a different accent to understand, and different customs for just about everything (no tipping—yay, if you're a student!). I visited castles and lochs, swam with Nessie, ate traditional dinners of haggis, neeps and tatties, drank beer—lots of beer—and made some amazing friends.

In the pub one meet-and-greet night with my fellow international student friends, I was speaking French to a girl from Bordeaux who, learning I was from North Vancouver, said, "You must meet Sean!" and she hauled me over to meet Sean, a guy from my hometown, who went to school with a couple of my friends.

One of my first weekends in Scotland I joined my new, from-my-hometown friend Sean, along with his two flatmates, Scott and Paul, on a trip to the Isle of Arran, just off the west coast. We sat together on the train and the ferry, and once on the island, took a short bus ride up to the castle, where we took a tour around the old mansion, and then decided to head off into the fields to explore.

The map we had was very simple—basically a not-to-scale cartoon map of the grounds, with a simple view of the few walking trails. After walking along the trails for a bit, we got bored, and decided to go into the forest. The underbrush was pretty thick, and we quickly got lost and figured it might be a good idea to veer back towards civilization, since absolutely no one on Earth knew where we were. Deciding to again be adventurous, we cut across a large field, and then had to jump two fences to get back to the path we could see waaaay over there. To finish off our Scottish countryside adventure, we jumped a couple more fences to get up close and personal with the hairy highland coos (cows). Scott and Sean got extra close for a picture—unfortunately the only one I managed to take is of them hightailing it away from the menacing horns of the cow!

Our adventures continued over the course of the semester as we kept exploring our new country. We also became a great support system for each other. Just a few weeks into the term, we had created a wonderful family of friends from all over the world. As we went to classes, did our homework, shared meals and went shopping together, we found we could lean on each other for support, encouragement, a shoulder to cry on, and a friend who would listen and not judge.

Exhilarated by my experience, I planned to spend the spring of 2007 in Europe backpacking with my boyfriend at the time. We arrived in Istanbul with our bags, cameras, debit cards, train passes and no set plans. Only 48 hours into our trip, we realized we'd made a huge mistake; it was still too early in the season to take the tourist ferries from Istanbul to the Greek Islands! Wandering around Sultanahmet, we found a small travel agency and told them our plight. After the travel agent finished laughing at us, he fixed us up with a great three-day itinerary that would take us down the coast to the only functioning ferry port and let us see some of Turkey's greatest sites. Continuing the trip after this small hiccup, and making sure to keep on rolling with the punches, we enjoyed the next ten weeks, travelling across the continent all the way to Ireland, following our whims and taking whichever train left the station next. My first true backpacking experience had me hooked.

Back in Vancouver, broke, and finally graduated, I endured a year of domestication—moved in with the boyfriend, held down an apartment, returned to my office job and started my next degree. It didn't take long to realize I was miserable. So I left the guy, quit the job, moved home to my parents and started looking for my next adventure. Needing a few more credits to finish off degree number two, I decided to head back across the pond to join a good friend in Greece for an archaeology field school. Our 14-week program included a week's orientation in Athens before the big move to a beautiful Greek island to learn the language, eat the food, dance to traditional music and, oh yeah, dig up an ancient cemetery and earn a few credits while we were at it.

Someone had generously decided that we might need a week's break from our already idyllic lifestyle, and I was lucky enough to have the opportunity to spend ten days in Egypt and fulfill a lifelong dream of seeing the pyramids. The week and a half that I spent there opened my eyes to traditions and cultures that were the most unlike my own I had ever encountered. I visited a Nubian village, sailed down the Nile, rode a camel through the Sahara desert at sunset and met some truly amazing people that week, making memories that I will certainly never forget. For me, this trip sealed the deal. I needed to travel. My dreams of becoming a history professor could be put on hold: academia would be there when I got back; I wouldn't always be in my mid-twenties! Our tour leader, Dave, had left New Zealand four years earlier in search of work and a life abroad, and had never looked back. I figured I could do the same, and promised myself that one day I would give it a try.

Back in Vancouver, I got a good job, paid off all my student debt, and saved as much as I could. In October 2010, at the age of 26, I set off with a few one-way tickets for however long it took to see as much of the world as I could. Over the next 18 months, I visited ten countries on five continents. I spent time with the Big Five in South Africa, and dived to the depths of the Indian and Atlantic Oceans. I visited the highest country in the world in Lesotho, and spent nights in grass huts in Mozambique. I saw the birthplace of Freddie Mercury in Zanzibar, and made it to the Roof of Africa by trekking up Kilimanjaro in Tanzania. A series of jobs in Australia, from picking grapes by hand to running the service desk at an IT firm, allowed me to make enough money to visit the highlights of every state and territory on the continent, and I made it out of Oz with hours to spare on my visa to the rice paddies of Bali, Indonesia. A stop to see a friend in San Francisco, and I was home to regroup and start planning the next phase of my life.

While I was in South Africa, I had started scuba diving, beginning with just a very basic Discover Scuba Diving course that let me do two dives to a depth of 12 meters with an instructor. I loved it. On my first dive I saw sharks, massive lobsters, moray eels, and fish I never knew existed. On the boat trip back to shore, I saw a mother humpback whale and her calf breaching and playing in the water. Completely captivated, I took my first two certifications in Cape Town and immediately took a dive vacation to Mozambique.

Over a summer in Vancouver, I realized that I could combine my new passion with a career; I could become a professional diver, and make a living doing the two things I loved the most. In October 2012, I headed to the island of Tortola, in the British Virgin Islands, to take the PADI Divemaster course, the first professional level of recreational scuba diving. I spent long days in the sun, water and waves, logging hours on the bottom of the sea and lots more on land, filling tanks, rinsing and sorting gear; I learned something new every day.

I've now spent the last 22 months travelling sandy shores from the Caribbean to the Middle East working along the way as a Divemaster. Logging another few hundred dives and hours underwater, my hair turned blonde by unending hours in the salt water and sunshine, and I've managed to do all right for myself. I don't have a lot of money, but I have a lot of fantastic memories. I've been to 30 countries, dived on five continents, and rarely ever look back to wish I'd done something differently.

One thing that hasn't changed, from that very first chance I took by going to Scotland eight years ago, is that it's not always easy. It's not easy to leave everything you know behind—your friends, your family, your job, your home, your life—and start anew. I still feel that every time I move, every time I go to a new place, I am starting again. In a lot of ways, this is fantastic, because I get to reinvent myself; I get to be a newer, and hopefully better version of myself, and show this person to those around me.

Sometimes, you manage to find a place where you just feel like you were meant to be. I've had a few of these experiences before, most recently in the summer of 2013 in Amorgos, Greece. In these kinds of places you make great friends quickly, become part of social circles easily, engage in cultural activities with local people often, and generally love being there. I fit into life on Amorgos like one of those round pegs.

My time spent in Greece previously and my small grasp of the language helped me settle in easily and make friends with plenty of locals. On my first day on the island, I met the owner of a local restaurant, and we discovered our mutual love of ouzo. Almost every night after that, whether the restaurant was busy or not, my spot at a little table under the window was reserved, and we spent hours drinking this traditional liquor, listening to live Greek music and talking about everything we could think of, often surrounded by other friends from the village. Enclosed in the small square of the white-walled, blue-doored village, it was the closest to being a local I've ever felt.

Many times I've had people tell me how amazing my life is, how it always seems perfect, and how incredibly lucky I am that I seem to have fallen from the sky and landed myself in yet another dream destination. What a lot of people don't see is that travelling, and especially travelling and working, is not a vacation for me. It is not always glamorous and perfect and Facebook profile picture worthy. There are late nights, early mornings, long days, endless time zones, long flights, bus trips, train trips, walks, masses of details and schedule changes that somehow need to fit together to make this kind of life work. I have cried, a lot, at times and that is okay. It means that I still respect the enormity of what I'm trying to accomplish—travel the world.

It has been hard work to constantly make decisions that at any moment could change my life, but to be able to deal with it, to be able to cope with living in the moment, I needed to just let go. It's very difficult, especially for someone like me who always likes to be in control, but I find when I can just let things happen, the best things happen. For me, part of just letting go is forgiving myself for seemingly bad decisions I've made in the past. I can truly say that I have no regrets. Sure, not every decision I've made has been a good one, but I've been able to learn from every mistake and wrong turn I've made. The lessons, though often hard to swallow, and not always immediately clear, are what make the challenges of travelling so rewarding.

Not every decision can lead to the desired or expected outcome. Often when travelling, I have been let down because of unrealistic expectations. Over the years, I've learned to try to have as little expectation as possible, so that I'm less surprised when things go differently than planned, and more importantly, I'm less disappointed when I go to a new place. Putting it in these terms sounds harsh, but really it's about opening my mind up to experience a wide range of possibilities. Everyone views things differently, so to expect that I would be just as wowed by the Duomo as my best friend was, is unrealistic. For the record, she almost cried; I almost walked right past it.

Of course, I didn't get to this point alone. Everyone needs a support system, and the kind of support that I have found while travelling is as non-traditional as it gets. I have met some very incredible people over the years. Some of these people I am still in touch with, others have faded away, but all of them have had an impact. We have laughed and cried and shared stories over food and drink, compared memories of places visited and talked about journeys we hoped to make. We have made plans to meet up that we never intended to follow, and sometimes ran into each other again on the other side of the world. Even when travelling alone, it's difficult for me to be lonely.

While I'm on the road, and even while I'm semi-settled in a place far from home, there are people who are my support system, and I am theirs. On a train in Australia, I met a lovely girl from England who was also going to Perth. We exchanged numbers, and made plans to meet up at the beach in a few days' time. The night before we were supposed to meet, my boyfriend called from 3,000 kilometers away and told me he wanted to call it quits. I was heart-broken, but didn't want to cancel my plans with Elle as I knew it would be the last chance we had to meet up. I called her to say that even though I would still make it, I probably wouldn't be very good company. She instantly said, "You need chocolate," and asked me my favourite kind. She brought me a chocolate bar, took me for ice cream, and made me smile for the entire afternoon. Even though we've lost touch, I still sometimes think of the incredible support and kindness she showed a fellow traveller in need.

I know that I am incredibly lucky to also have the unwavering support of my parents and sister. My parents have never asked me to stop travelling and "get a real job." They have always wanted me to be happy, even if that means being dirt poor and very far from home. They have encouraged me to take chances, big and small, and continue to support my wild and crazy ideas, and my ever changing plans.

The further I continue along this journey of life, the more I realize that so many of my successes on the road were set up before I ever left home. My parents made sure I got a good education, earning my high school diploma and encouraging me to go to university. Though I don't directly use either of my degrees, indirectly they have benefitted me immensely. The communication skills that we learn in the education system are invaluable, and have helped me gain employment and make friends around the world.

My parents also made sure I knew the value of a dollar: I had to fund my first-ever trip to Europe myself when I was 15. I got a job and worked all summer long just to save up the money for it. While my friends from school spent their money hand over fist for the ten days we were in Germany and France, my sister and I were careful with our choices—we knew how many hours of work went into buying that baguette. Even now, double the age I was when I first went to Europe, I still count my pennies to make them last longer.

If I'd told my 20-year-old self what I'd be doing at 30, I certainly wouldn't have believed me. As I look towards my next decade of life, I really don't know what to expect, but the experiences I've lived through have prepared me to just accept whatever comes my way. Hopefully, by sharing my experiences I can open a door to a world that you might not even know exists.

The world is at once a very big and a very small place, but no matter which way you look at it, there are opportunities to take advantage of and memories to be made in every wide-open plain as well as hidden cave. I hope that I can continue to find these places, explore them, and keep being surprised by where I end up. The best advice I can give is really a series of things you've heard time and time again: dream big, follow your heart, and don't be afraid to make mistakes. Whatever you choose to do, wherever your path takes you, it will never be easy, but the challenges you overcome will make it all the more rewarding.

NJ

As a high school teacher, in May and June I witness students starting their journey to what many of them call their 'real' lives, and every year I listen to their concerns as well as their dreams. Inevitably one or two of them ask my advice about what they should do, or how I would handle any number of situations. I am often reticent to offer my opinions, as each student has taken a different path to this particular place in time and this decision in their life. Some struggle with personal issues, some struggle with academic issues, some seemingly have no struggles at all. One thing I am confident sharing is that every event is simply what we make of it. We can choose how we see and experience life. Each part of our journey teaches us about our beliefs and ourselves.

To understand who we are to become we must embrace each aspect of our journey, good or bad. Success often means surviving and learning from what is placed in our path. The journey to who we are, and how we face this journey, is the most important determining factor in our success. To understand who we are we must embrace how we got there.

I grew up in a small town, with your typical small town values, but above all they valued sameness, essentially the ability to blend. Being like everyone else was imperative; however, I was a square peg trying to fit in a round hole. As a child I watched how people fit together, and tried to emulate what I saw to little or no avail. How they interacted, formed friendships, and just generally got along was a mystery. I knew the mechanics, and what was supposed to happen, but never quite seemed to be able to put the pieces together for myself. In short, making friends was next to impossible.

To make matters worse, school was equally challenging. Once again I knew what was supposed to happen, and in my head it made perfect sense, but on paper, well that was a different matter. Words and numbers seemed to meld together into an incomprehensible jumble. I knew that I understood what was being expected and could do it, but it seemed that no one else did. So, as time went on it became easier to be known as the bad kid instead of the stupid kid.

To say I had a tumultuous relationship with the school establishment would be an understatement. It is interesting when you look back and try to determine the moments in your life that truly matter. What makes them different from all the rest?

I believe it is the moments you decide you matter. Your belief in you takes precedence above all else, and while that might seem simplistic, it is the very essence of personal success. Belief in yourself and your abilities. One of those defining moments happened for me when I stood in my principal's office hearing once again that I was stupid, I would not amount to much, and I would be lucky to graduate high school. I simply turned around, left the office, and ran home in my stocking feet in the middle of winter. Deep down I knew that I was not what she was saying. I knew that I was something more that.

One intrinsic belief that I inherited from my parents was a respect for authority—to not only be respectful, but accepting and unquestioning. I never told anyone about my time in the principal's office as I thought no one would believe me. A chance encounter with another authority figure changed my life, and as luck would have it, another principal. What I thought was a chat with yet another person trying to fix my bad behaviour, really was what we now call an educational assessment. During this session it was discovered that I had a learning disability, and a rather severe one at that. Instead of berating and belittling me, this principal believed and battled for me. Now my difference had a name, and I hoped maybe even a way to make me normal and once we fixed it I would be like everyone else. For the next several years I was taught how to train my brain to process information so that I could read and write. I was fortunate as my innate ability for problem solving allowed me to create strategies to learn what was expected.

Many people ask me what it is like to have a learning disability, and I describe it one of two ways. First, it is like when you are asked a question you know the answer, but you just cannot figure it out. It is frustrating and annoying. Imagine that all the time without any resolution. Second, is being part of a game where everyone knows the rules, but you. Everyone knows how to behave, what to say, and what to do, but part of the game is to make sure that you never figure out how to play. You can watch, and play, even ask questions, but you will never be part of the game.

What most people do not understand is that many people with learning disabilities also have difficulty reading social cues. What that means for me is that I often misinterpret social situations, and as a result inadvertently act inappropriately. While some situations have resulted in amusing stories, others have resulted in lost friends and even being fired. When you are unaware of how people are reacting to your words and actions it is nearly impossible to rectify any mistakes you might make.

Never one to back down from a challenge, I spent years in socialization training and completing nightly exercises to ensure that I could read and write better than most. One of my greatest assets is the ability to look at a problem, break it down into manageable parts, and create a solution that generally everyone can understand. This is one positive skill that my learning disability allowed me to cultivate. This skill also made me well suited for jobs in the fields of marketing, public relations and fundraising; ironically all of these professions require an inordinate amount of interaction in various social situations.

While my skills were well suited to these professions, I was not. I struggled to understand what I was doing wrong as I could do the job, but somehow something was always wrong. I did not connect with the client, I said something wrong, or I simply did not understand what was expected. From the outside I looked successful, it looked like I had it all together, but the truth is I went through six jobs in under five years. Some I left before I was let go, and others, well let's just say we did not part ways on a positive note. With each setback came the doubt, the self-loathing and the depression. What was it that I had to do to be really successful?

While very few of these experiences were positive, there was one boss who recognized my need for guidance. Yes he did fire me, but he insisted as part of my severance package that we meet a month after my termination to discuss what had occurred. In our final interview he took the time to explain to me the obstacles to my success. He simply stated that I was trying so hard to fit in that I never really listened to what people were saying. I was like a bulldozer with an agenda, something to complete and no one was going to get in my way. I listened, but I never really heard what was being said. He also noted, that although I had the skills, and could learn how to interact with clients, I was never really happy or excited about what I was doing. It appeared that I was going through the motions, doing what was expected, but not what was needed. This was not easy to hear, and it took a long time for me to process this information, but when I was ready I understood what he was saying. I was so determined to prove everyone wrong that I did not understand that every interaction is a reciprocal relationship. Meaning, each party needs to feel that they have received something of value from the relationship; the one key discovery I never quite understood despite years of socialization training.

It took failure, and lots of it, for me to understand that if you do not feel that you are understood, listened to and valued then all the right words, or actions mean nothing. It took me a while to understand what this actually meant. How in my life could I make the changes necessary to positively move forward?

This guidance provided me with an opportunity to examine my life, and consciously decide what my next step would be. Over the years I had applied to Teacher's College and not been accepted. I never wanted another child to feel as worthless as I had, but something always seemed to get in the way of achieving this goal. This was a profession that I had never really strayed far from as I had always volunteered as a tutor for students with learning disabilities. Being a teacher, was what I had dreamed of, but had given up on. I decided to apply one last time and let fate choose what my future would be. I would accept the outcome and move in whatever direction the universe pointed me.

I was accepted to teacher's college.

I now have a career—or maybe calling is a better word—that I love. That being said, I am now part of a profession that is extremely hard to succeed in, at least in the conventional manner. Many cuts have been made to the education system, and this is reflected in fewer teachers and larger classroom sizes, and because of this every year in May or June I am either laid-off or reassigned. This has made me re-evaluate what it means to be successful. I certainly am not where I expected to be at this point in my life.

When I was 20, I felt that I would be working a job that provided a steady income, have some idea of where I was heading and essentially be settled into a life that would be comfortable. My reality is far from my 20-year-old self's vision. Every month is a struggle as I do not have a job that is reliable. I have to think about how the bills will get paid and worry that I may have to adjust my lifestyle, and may have to leave a job I love for purely financial reasons. I find that this struggle only serves to make the successes even sweeter.

When I look back there are a few pieces of wisdom that I wish I had realized early on in my journey as I believe these revelations would have allowed me to learn more readily from my mistakes and perhaps even decreased many of the negative thoughts I had. There are moments that I would change, but I wonder if I did would I be a different person.

The journey, however difficult, should be savoured. Each experience provides you with knowledge that allows you to make better choices along the way.

If you allow the mistakes to rule your life, you cause yourself needless angst. Success does not come overnight, and while this might seem cliché, the journey is more important than the destination.

Without the pitfalls, errors and missteps it is hard to recognize when things go right. Embrace the errors and take them for what they are—an opportunity to learn. Do not berate yourself or dwell on all the things you have done wrong because everyone makes mistakes.

Mentors, bosses and teachers who are valuable will understand and accept your imperfections, and instead of using them as weapons, will use them as tools for improvement. If these are not the kind of people you have in your life, then you need to find them.

The learning moments are important. It is hard to hear that we are not doing a good job, or that we are subpar, but we need to look at these moments as the most important aspects of our learning process, because if we do not we are simply doomed to continue to fail.

Only through recognition of failure can we determine what success is. Even though I may not know what will happen next month, or heck even next week, I know that I have learned from my mistakes and am working on making tomorrow better than yesterday.

As a teacher I am constantly assessing my lessons, my behaviour and interaction with students. Am I perfect? Absolutely not. Are there things that I would do differently? Absolutely yes. Does that mean that I am not successful? I believe that it is the exact opposite. It means that I am successful because the heart of success is making us better people and learning from each experience.

When I was 20 I thought that being successful meant earning a lot of money and holding a job that was prestigious. Now in my forties I realize that success is simply about being a better person. It is about internalizing what and who you want to be and working towards that goal each day.

External validation should not be the determining factor in your success. While it is rewarding to hear a student tell you that you made a difference in their life, or that you helped them believe in their abilities, recognition should not be your sole purpose. You need to be able to determine your own success, because nobody else can.

I once received a fortune cookie that read *"follow your bliss."* I still keep this in my wallet and for a long time I did not think that this would happen for me. I may not be there yet, and my journey to bliss may take me longer than expected. I now know that dead ends, detours and wrong turns are simply steppingstones to success. Being the person that I want to be and who I was meant to be is success.

NICKY

Looking back on my childhood, you could say my calling was obvious, but the path to my dreams took many twists and turns. I was 35 before I realised what I really wanted to do in life, before I found a job that fulfilled me both intellectually and emotionally.

My story begins in third-world Africa, in a city then known as Salisbury, the capital of Rhodesia. Back in 1973 it was a country at war, the white minority-run government having declared a Unilateral Declaration of Independence (UDI) from Britain in 1965. Seven years after my birth, in 1980, the war was over, and Robert Mugabe took control of the newly independent Zimbabwe. To me it was just home, and being taught the dos and don'ts of hand grenades and land mines under the big old monkey-rope tree in the school grounds was part and parcel of life.

Compared to the majority of children growing up in Zimbabwe, my childhood was one of privilege. Our home was spacious and set in an acre of garden which Mum kept green, lush, and full of flowers. It was a paradise in which my sister and I spent hours creating secret fairy gardens. My other childhood passions included cutting pretty pictures out of magazines and collaging them onto boards, doing woodwork projects with my brother in Dad's workshop, playing with clay in my granny's studio, or crafting a home for my precious Cindy doll. As I got older I used to love rearranging my bedroom, trying to find the best use of space.

My mum tells a story of waking in the night to find my sister and me diligently rearranging our dolls on the shelves of the kitchen pantry, while the contents of the pantry shelves were relocated to the dolls' cupboard in our bedroom, using the doll's pram as transport!

Looking back, a thread of creativity was woven through my childhood, but along the way I was diverted from the course. It didn't help that I was bright academically, and, according to the results of my first psychometric testing at age 16, capable of pursuing almost any career I wanted to. But at that time my vision was clouded by expectation and convention, and I didn't fully understand my passion.

Being clever can have a downside, too, and school holds mixed memories for me. I was hopeless at sport, ridiculed for my faith, teased for wearing glasses, and kissing me was generally considered a punishment for the guys playing spin-the-bottle. As a result, my self-esteem took a battering, and I was always acutely aware of what I thought other people thought of me.

Another significant factor in my career choice was the lack of female role models. I was born into a society that was racially segregated. When I was a child, white women were mothers, teachers, doctors and nurses. They worked in shops and travel agencies, or became secretaries or sales reps. Black women were maids and nannies, or sold tomatoes and crochet doilies at the side of the road.

My own mum, forced by my gran's snobbishness to go to university, had studied physiotherapy, seeing it as an easier option than medicine. Mum's calling was the stage, but she was not allowed to pursue such a vulgar vocation—"because everyone knows what goes on backstage!" Mum stopped working when my younger brother was born and, for the rest of my childhood, was a stay-at-home mum.

Dad, on the other hand, had not gone to university, but wished he had. Instead he left school at 17 and, in his search for adventure, joined the British South Africa Police (BSAP) and was posted out to Rhodesia shortly before UDI was declared. On leaving the police,

Dad eventually started a picture framing business, which grew to employ around 80 workers.

Dad's business was very much a part of my childhood; I used to love spending days at the factory when on school holidays. As I got older I was allowed to help customers choose frames for their pictures, which gave me a real buzz. This experience quietly sowed seeds of inspiration as I was growing up. It steered my choice of degree course, introduced me to the possibility of becoming an entrepreneur and instilled in me an appreciation of art.

As a teenager I found myself at one of the best girls' high schools in Zimbabwe, generally referred to as the "Pink Prison." Arundel was a very competitive academic environment, offering subjects considered "suitable for young ladies," and our headmistress, Miss Twiss, kept a tight rein over her girls. Because I wasn't very good at still life painting, I was told that I was no good at art and made to study dressmaking instead. If only I had realised then that art comes in many guises, only one of which is still life painting. But, lacking in self-esteem, I didn't challenge the opinions of those in authority.

What the school lacked was decent career guidance. It was all very well excelling at maths and English literature, but I had no understanding of what career choices this opened up for me. If I could turn back the clock I might have chosen to study architecture, but I had no exposure to this career as a child.

As a family we holidayed regularly within Zimbabwe, and every couple of years made the three-day drive down to South Africa for beach holidays. I can remember, on those drives, spending hours transfixed by the passing landscapes, the tranquillity of big open spaces, and nature's inspirations in colour, texture and pattern. My eyes were not opened to the world outside of Southern Africa until my first trip overseas when I was 15.

By the time I had written my O-levels at age 16, I was tired of being pushed academically, and had no desire to go on to university. I had dreams of becoming a London version of Melanie Griffiths in *Working Girl*. My parents agreed, but on the condition that I at least finished my A-levels, which would qualify me for university should I ever change my mind. This meant selecting just three subjects, considerably narrowing my options. I eventually settled on maths, biology and accounting, which I felt would keep my options open for a career in the sciences or business worlds, but began to close the door on my creative aspirations. At the same time I studied typing and bookkeeping so that I was qualified to work as a secretary once I finished school.

In my final year of high school my parents decided to move the family to the UK so that my younger sister and brother could attend British universities at local student rates (and not at the hideously expensive rates for foreign students). So, at age 18, I had a decision to make: did I move with the family, or did I stay in Zimbabwe? After years of looking after my mother, who hadn't been well, and feeling the need to escape the strict rules of my parents, I felt that freedom would be found as far away from them as possible—and 6,000 miles seemed like a good distance.

I moved in with family friends who had a spare room and found a job as a personal assistant to the manager of a foam manufacturing company. I had the use of Mum's old car and financial independence, and I had a ball as I found my feet as a young adult. And so the next stage of my life began. I was living my *Working Girl* dream—but in Harare instead of London. Though I was good at my job, I wasn't passionate about it and I was soon bored and in need of a new challenge.

It was a position in a leather company that caught my eye, a job that would combine my organisational skills with something a bit more creative. However, my parents had been encouraging me to move to the UK, or at least to visit them on holiday, so I decided to fit in a trip between jobs. I'm not quite sure what happened, but before I knew it I was living and working as a secretary in the UK and my dream job in the leather company never came to fruition. Perhaps if I had returned to Zimbabwe and taken up that job I might have found my calling sooner than I did, but it is impossible to know what might have been on another path.

After a couple more years of secretarial work, I realised that I needed to take action, and that maybe university was the right option after all. I still didn't really know what I wanted to do but I had a naïve notion that science subjects would lead to higher earnings in future. Guided by my science and business A-Levels, and feeling an affinity to the manufacturing industry from my dad's business, I chose a course that I thought would suit my needs—Manufacturing Engineering with Business Studies.

Looking back now, I realise that I hated statistics and the mechanical side of engineering, but I loved learning about ergonomics, the product design process, Maslow's hierarchy of needs and the psychology of marketing and management. And, with my organisational skills, I thoroughly enjoyed learning how to make processes super-efficient.

While I was at university my parents' marriage ended. Mum had returned to Zimbabwe a couple of years earlier, and when the divorce finally came through she decided to sell our beautiful home in Harare and move out to Zimbabwe's remote Eastern Highlands where she bought 32 acres of land. Her vision was to create an oasis for local tourists. It was an exciting venture, and gave her a new lease on life as she took on the challenge of building a house for herself and accommodation for guests, as well as landscaping the grounds.

I travelled out to Zimbabwe during our long summer, and got stuck into helping Mum design, build and furnish her new home. I spent days with a team of workers, thinning trees in the forests or creating a path down to the river that fronted her property. We drove to the hardware shop in the nearest town, an hour away, to choose bathroom fittings or windows. We bought meters of fabric from the haberdashery which I sewed into duvet covers and pillow cases. Our days were busy, but I loved what I was doing and time passed effortlessly.

Dad, too, picked up the pieces of his life and met and married Jenny. They also moved back to Zimbabwe, where he still owned his business. However, with the deteriorating economic situation in my beloved country, running his business was becoming increasingly difficult. They packed up their life there and moved to Australia where they bought a picture framing and art gallery business near the Glass House Mountains in Queensland.

I learnt a valuable lesson during those days when Mum recounted the story of South African Alison Botha who had been interviewed on TV. When she was just 24, Alison was abducted from outside her home in Port Elizabeth by two men who raped, stabbed and disembowelled her. They slashed her throat multiple times and left her for dead. But Alison wasn't dead, and somehow, with her throat slit and her intestines in her hands, she managed to crawl to the side of the road where she eventually flagged down help.

Alison's ethos is that you might not be able to control your circumstances, but you can control your Attitude, your Beliefs and your Choices—her A, B, C mantra for life. Although it took me a while to act on her advice, her words stuck with me and slowly infiltrated my decisions.

As my three years at university came to an end I was determined to leave with a good job offer. The most logical option was to apply to join a graduate training scheme in the manufacturing industry. It never crossed my mind to try something different after all my hard work. In my final year, I pushed myself to complete application after application, and then interview after interview. It was exhausting, but the effort paid off and I left university with three job offers. I remember calling Mum in Zimbabwe and her advice to me was to go for the job where I felt I would have the most fun—a mindset I embraced. It was sound advice, but I hadn't realised the importance for me to enjoy my work, and not just what happens outside work hours.

I decided to accept a job offer at Ford Motor Company. The

job was in the IT department—not what I wanted, but a foot in the door of a company with a large graduate programme, offering prospects of a lively social life for new recruits such as me. As much as I did not enjoy my time in IT, the experience I gained has been invaluable. As soon as I was able, I transferred from IT into the engineering department, where I spent the next seven years designing and installing production lines to make engine components. I could do my job well, but I never did discover a passion for achieving a three micron roundness tolerance on a crankshaft.

The upside of my time at Ford was that with a reasonable salary I could afford to travel. I also started dating Dave, whose cultural upbringing and sense of eccentric style helped awaken my creative spirit. Together we travelled to Barcelona, where I fell in love with Gaudi's quirky architecture. I noticed the decorated pavements and the carved wooden doors. Suddenly a new world opened up to me. A world that, growing up in a country whose architectural history only dated back about 100 years, had never really crossed my mind. I was transfixed!

Italy was our next destination where I saw first-hand the Leaning Tower of Pisa, Michelangelo's David, and his paintings in the Sistine Chapel. History was coming alive for me, and it was exhilarating.

We travelled to the Caribbean where I discovered the joys of scuba diving and the beauty and tranquility of the underwater world, the vibrant colours of reef fish and the patterns of coral. The more I travelled, the more I wanted to travel. I wanted to learn about other cultures and traditions, taste different foods, immerse myself in new and exciting experiences.

Then into my life came Pippa, the wife of one of my engineering colleagues, and a complete breath of fresh air. Pippa had studied art history at university, and then trained as a chef under Pru Leith. She is bubbly and vivacious, and we hit it off immediately. We discovered a shared love of books and introduced each other to our favourite authors. Pippa took me to art galleries and exhibitions, stately houses and gardens. I began to realise just how much I'd been craving this world.

I celebrated my 30th birthday with a rip-roaring 1920s party. But inside I knew that I was stuck in a comfortable financial rut. Suddenly the thought of my tombstone reading "Nicola had a successful career at Ford Motor Company" was beginning to feel decidedly unappealing. Surely there was more to life than that? The adventure spark in me had been lit and I wanted more.

Coincidentally, Ford was looking to reduce its headcount and was offering its employees sabbaticals, which meant that I would have the security of a job to come back to. I jumped at this opportunity to travel. I remortgaged my flat to raise the funds, and eventually persuaded Dave, now my ex but still a very good friend, to come with me. We spent a year on the road, visiting 26 countries across four continents.

We started off in the relative safety of Africa, landing in Nairobi, Kenya and then travelling overland south through Eastern and Southern Africa. I particularly loved the islands off the coasts of Kenya and Tanzania. They are a melting pot of cultures, harking back to the days of spice trading between Persia, India and East Africa. The narrow, cobbled lanes boast intricately carved doorways from Arabia and India, and a heady mix of spices and flavours from these combined cultures.

From Africa we flew to Nepal and India, where I was struck by total sensory overload—the sights, sounds, tastes and smells. I found it thrilling! The architectural style and embellishments were like nothing I'd ever seen before. I was overwhelmed, not just with the beauty but also the complexity of the design and building, especially considering the tools and technology that would have been available at the time. Our next stops were Southeast Asia, then Bali and Japan. Each country was so different, but wonderful in its own unique way. I've lost count of how many hundreds of pictures I took along the way. With my new digital SLR camera I was also discovering the art of photography.

After an interlude in Australia and New Zealand, where our focus turned back to nature, we then headed for South America—another completely different culture. I discovered the marvels of Macchu Pichu, the clay city of Chan Chan, and the brightly colourful Andean fabrics. After a few days in Rio it was time to return to the grey of an English winter—back to earth with a bump!

I arrived home willing Ford to make me redundant so that I could move my life onto a different path, but instead they found me another job, right back in my old department. I was gutted, but at least I would be able to pay the bills. And, they wanted me to train as a Six Sigma Black Belt. At the time my intention was to complete the training then find myself a high-powered and well-paid job in the city and finally fulfil my dream of working and living in London.

But life has a habit of throwing in curve balls every now and then. His name was Nick, and I met him internet dating. Soon after meeting Nick, he was offered a six-month sabbatical from work, and his brother and I persuaded him that travelling would be a good thing to do. He agreed and asked if I'd like to be his personal guide. How could I say no to that? I was already in the process of looking for a new job, so the decision to leave Ford, once and for all, was an easy one to make, despite my colleagues' protestations about the loss of my pension. And, knowing that I wanted to end up in London when I got back, I had no hesitation in selling the flat that I loved in order to fund my travels.

A funny thing happens to you when you burn your bridges—it helps to focus the mind more clearly. As long as you maintain the safety net it's too easy to take the well-trodden path. During this second trip there were three incidents that, combined, totally changed the course of my life.

Our trip, and our souvenir shopping, started in Zanzibar, off the coast of Tanzania. By the time we reached my aunt in South Africa, having travelled through Tanzania, Zimbabwe and Mozambique, our bags were considerably heavier. As I was showing my aunt all our wonderful purchases she remarked that I really ought to find myself a job that involved buying nice things for other people. Light bulb moment number one.

Australia was our next stop, where we spent a couple of weeks with Dad before criss-crossing that vast continent. Dad's gallery held a magnetic attraction for me, and I found great joy in simply spending time there, surrounded by the art and crafts. Light bulb moment number two.

In Hong Kong, en-route to Southeast Asia, we popped into Nick's firm's offices, and I distinctly remember feeling a rising panic as we stepped out of the lift into the office space, with its fluorescent lighting and little cubicles. At that moment I knew that I could not go back to working in a big office like this. Light bulb moment number three.

By the time I arrived back on British soil I was craving a career that involved something much more creative—the only question was, what? I took some time out, reading, soul searching and brainstorming, and eventually settled on the idea of moving into interior design. But how would I go about making this transition? I was 35 and had no formal qualifications in this field. I did, however, have six years' experience in efficient space planning, an understanding of ergonomics, the ability to project manage, some invaluable IT experience, and plenty of skills in office management from my secretarial days. I also had an innate understanding of colour and texture, and an eye for arranging things beautifully.

My initial forays into how to go about working in interior design were not very successful, and one person even told me that I shouldn't bother trying. This was like a red rag to a bull. I was not going to take no for an answer! I took what I considered to be the easy route—I started my own business.

I've had many people tell me how brave that decision was, but what did I have to lose? I didn't have a job anyway. The sensible way to start a business is with some savings behind you, but I had just spent most of my savings. Instead I had Nick's backing, both financially and emotionally. Starting up the company didn't cost that much, and with a few short courses, lots of other transferrable skills and Nick's steadfast support, I was on my way to a career that I love—one that makes me jump out of bed most mornings.

The road to becoming an entrepreneur hasn't always been easy. There have been plenty of potholes and roadblocks along the way, but there is not a day that goes by when I wish I hadn't taken the risk. My life feels so much richer doing something fulfilling and, even though I have less money, I have abundance in my life because my need to be immersed in beauty and creativity is being met.

Six years on, with my business going from strength to strength and with hindsight on my side, my journey seems crystal clear. But in the middle of it, without an obvious path, it often felt confusing. Getting to where I am today has taken courage and determination; but luck and fortune have also played their part. I have been blessed by the opportunities and experiences that have helped me along the way. I was born into financial privilege, I was given a first-class education, and with these things the assumption and confidence that I would be able to succeed at something in life.

Understanding that my journey is influenced by my attitude, my beliefs and my choices, I always ask myself two questions when faced with a tough decision: What is the worst that could happen? What is the best that could happen?

It is too easy to focus on what could go wrong, and blow it out of all proportion, rather than focusing on what could go right. Often the greatest thing that holds us back is NOT making the decision to do something. Once you've decided to go for it, the rest somehow falls into place. In Zimbabwe we have a wonderful expression—"Make a plan." It's surprising what happens when you stop drifting and take action.

And so I thought I would end my story with the words of wisdom that I chose for myself to focus on this year:

- Taking time to live life will only inspire your work.

- Do what you love and do it often.
- If you change the way you look at things, the things you look at change.
- Hold the vision, trust the process.
- Be brave. Take risks. Nothing can substitute experience.
- When nothing goes right—go left.
- Non, je ne regrette rien.

Good luck with your journey!

ROB

Random thoughts of a 40-something dad, husband, and all-around boring guy.

What does a "20-something" want to know from a "40-something"? How the hell should I know? I'm just a guy minding my own business when one day I get an email from a friend asking if I would be a contributor to a project she's working on. It turned out to be the The20Project, and so here I am sitting in my front room typing madly away on my laptop. Did I mention the contribution is due in nine days? And that I've known about it for a few months? Ok, so first thing is, don't try to tell them not to procrastinate…

Maybe more importantly, don't "try to tell them" anything. What the hell did I think I could learn from somebody over 40 when I was in my twenties? Not very much. And who the hell am I to give advice? What qualifications do I have, other than not having died? As a parent, I learned long ago that my IQ in the eyes of my children started dropping as they got older, and hit rock bottom around the time they became teenagers.

In terms of generations, I'm a "bleeding-edge baby buster," meaning I was born right after the baby boom ended. I grew up in the 70s and 80s, when computers were just coming into homes. We had an Apple II+, as it was called, which is still in the basement of my parents' house. My high school had a "computer lab" where the smart kids got to learn to program in BASIC. At university, I learned drafting with a pencil and paper—three years later, my sister learned drafting on a computerized CAD program. I grew up worried about the USSR and nuclear war—today my kids have to worry about terrorism and dirty bombs. I'm not going to try to unpack the world's problems, but thanks to Hilary's prompt, I'll try to talk about some things I've learned in my 40-some years. So what have I learned?

I've learned it's not about me; it's about my legacy—my children.

I've learned that boring is good.

I've learned the importance of marrying well.

I've learned to have faith.

IT'S NOT ABOUT ME

I have two children, currently teenagers in high school. It seems that every time I turn around, they surprise me with their amazingness. In the middle of the worst day of my life, my children reminded me of what's really important.

On December 24, 1999, my wife and I got up and started to make breakfast. I put our 13-month-old daughter in her high chair, and then went to the TV room to play with our three-year-old son. The next thing I hear is the sound of water pouring on the floor, but I didn't react right away—until I heard my daughter screaming. I had put her in her high chair right next to the counter where my wife had put an electric kettle on for tea. Being a curious baby, she had pulled on the cord, turning the kettle over and dumping boiling water on her arm and side. All hell broke loose. Our son started yelling, our dog started barking, our daughter was screaming, and my wife and I were both charging into the kitchen from different directions.

I grabbed Aurora under her arms and started to pull, thinking the straps on her high chair would do what they do on TV—break. They didn't. I almost broke her legs trying to get her out of the chair. Meanwhile my wife turned the tap on in the sink, so once I took the straps off I could put her under cold running water. As a parent, you pretty quickly learn the difference between a shriek and a scream, and this was a scream. My daughter was in agony, and there was nothing I could do. My wife called 911 while I kept the water running and then grabbed ice from the fridge and threw it into the sink.

"Her skin's coming off!" I screamed while my wife tried to tell the 911 operator our address; our dog, Behr, barked nonstop, and our son kept asking, "What's wrong with Aurora?" I don't know how long it took the EMT to arrive at the house, but as soon as he did I wanted my wife to charge out the door with our daughter. Instead, he brought us inside the house and checked her out. He was only driving a Jeep Cherokee and was waiting for the ambulance to arrive. Once it did, they gave our daughter morphine and transported her to Alberta Children's Hospital. I packed our son into the truck and followed them. By the time I arrived, found a place to park, and figured out where she was, my little girl was wrapped in a burn bandage from her neck to her knees. Her left arm had taken the brunt of the water, but she had also been scalded on her side and her leg.

After a while in the ER, she was transferred to a room in the burn unit, and I decided to take my son out for lunch. As we were walking down the hall, it hit me what day it was and what this might mean for a three-year-old. I stopped to talk to him.

"Lorne, we have a problem. Aurora is going to have to stay in the hospital for a few days, and do you remember what tonight is?"

"Christmas Eve, Dad."

"That's right, so Santa is supposed to come to our house to bring presents."

I had to do some quick thinking.

"Lorne, what do you think should happen tonight? Should Santa come to drop off the presents, or should he wait until Aurora comes home? Santa gives moms and dads his cell phone number for emergencies like this."

I have never seen a more thoughtful expression than on that

child's face as he considered whether Santa Claus should bring presents or not. Eventually, he looked up at me and said, "Santa should wait until Aurora comes home."

I hadn't expected that answer—Lorne was really looking forward to his "Rescue Heroes" presents.

"Are you sure? Maybe Santa could make two trips?"

"NO, Daddy! Santa should wait until Aurora comes home."

He stomped his foot on the floor, a three-year-old boy insisting that his sister come home before Santa can bring him his presents. I cried as I took his hand, led him to the car, buckled him into his car seat, and took him to his grandma's house.

Aurora spent five days in the hospital, and Santa came to our house on the 28th that year. How does a three-year-old make a decision like that? What caused my little boy to give up on presents until his little sister was home safe?

That was the moment I knew it isn't about me, it's about my kids—who they become, how they behave, what they do. That's what I needed to focus on, not how much money I make or what kind of house I live in or what car I drive. As they have both grown, they have continued to demonstrate a wonderful degree of empathy and caring for others that still amazes me.

We live in Orange County, California. Yes, THAT Orange County. People here even refer to it as "the bubble," because we all realize it's not reality. The parking lot at the kids' school really is full of BMWs, Lexus, Mercedes, and the occasional Tesla. Sorry, I meant the STUDENT parking lot. So how do you keep your child grounded in that environment, where some of their classmates get to drive a Mercedes off the lot for their 16th birthday? My wife and I have done our best to do a couple of things:

1. Make sure they know what our priorities are (and it's not the latest outfit or the newest car).
2. Show them the reality that most people live in.

This will sound like a cliché, but our kids really do notice how we behave. They notice when we sponsor kids through World Vision or Compassion International. They notice when we volunteer at homeless shelters. They notice when my wife packs bags for homeless people in her truck and gives them out as she drives around to clients (she's a speech therapist who works with kids in their homes, and drives a few hundred miles a week). When we asked my son what he wanted to do for his 16th birthday, we were a bit shocked when he said he wanted to get a group of his friends and volunteer at the Orange County Rescue Mission. (His friends were even more shocked because he didn't tell them that was what they were doing until they arrived.J)

Living in Orange County, we are about two hours from Mexico. Just across the border, there is a town called El Nino, because it was created when a town on the coast was flooded during El Nino conditions about 15 years ago. The Mexican army packed the townspeople into trucks, drove them inland to a place just south of San Diego and dumped them on a hillside. There was no town, no services, no utilities, nothing. A number of charities and churches began working with the local people to help them, and one of the programs involved building houses. Long story short, a local resident has to acquire title to the land and then the charity or church raises the funds to purchase the building materials. A concrete pad is poured, and once it sets the volunteers trek to El Nino and build houses. We've been taking our kids down on these trips since they were in elementary school, and we could not imagine the effect. Seeing the joy on the children's faces when we brought them a football (meaning soccer here in the US), and seeing how little they have, really changed my children's perspectives. It seems condescending, but the "Mom, I want..." and "Dad, can I have..." requests from my kids disappeared for months after our first trip to El Nino. We've gone just about every year, and we've seen the improvements in the town since our first trip. Some of the streets are paved, there are stores and shops, and there's a market on Saturdays that is packed.

The most difficult part of taking the kids down there wasn't safety (there's no crime, since no one has anything); it was explaining to our kids why things were the way they were. Why did the people in El Nino have nothing? Why didn't they have schools and stores and jobs? Where were the mansions and fancy cars like we have at home? How do you explain global economics and geopolitics to an eight-year-old? You do your best. On many of our drives back from El Nino, I tried to explain why big companies like Honda were building car plants nearby but they weren't hiring everyone in the town, or why other companies were building huge tracts of housing for workers in their new factories instead of hiring the people from El Nino. There have been many times in my life where I've failed to do something, but none of them feel as bad as not being able to explain something to your children.

BORING IS GOOD

Throughout my life, society seems to have been chasing "more" or "crazier." I grew up learning to ski and skate. Then came snowboarding, freestyle and the X games, and the Olympics just had an event called "ski slopestyle." All of these events just seem to be wilder and crazier. I want people to think about the opposite—boring.

A couple of years ago I went for my annual physical (yes, men, after you turn 40 they insist on a digital exam that has nothing to do with computers...). My doctor walked into the room with my results, stopped, took a breath, and said, "I'm probably the only person who can say you're boring without being insulting."

When my eyebrow went up, he continued.

"Your results are almost exactly the same as last year—down to the decimal point."

And he turned the chart to show me that that was, in fact, the case. Blood pressure, cholesterol, PSA, etc, all the same as the year before. Granted, I'm very fortunate to be in that situation, but at the same time I have a pretty constant routine that includes going to the gym four or five days a week. Like I said, boring is good. No, I don't have a new workout program that will keep you in shape into your forties that I'll be happy to sell for $29.00 plus shipping and handling; I'm just suggesting you think about the boring, routine parts of your life that WILL keep you in shape into your forties. Put down the Xbox/PS3/whatever and get outside. Go for a walk or a jog or a run or a bike ride. Make it a habit, which means forcing yourself to do it for however many weeks it takes until you stop having to force yourself.

I've been going to a gym since my last year at university, which means I've been doing it for almost 25 years. I'm a morning person, so I tend to go early, before most people get there. It's usually pretty empty, so I'm not waiting for equipment. Gyms aren't everyone's bag, though, so get active. Facebook is full of memes about those of us who grew up in the seventies, how we were outside all the time, and we didn't come home until the streetlights came on. We're also the generation who got to play the very first video game (called *Pong*—look it up) so we probably started the trend toward sitting inside in front of a screen. I know the screen is exciting, but put it away for a while and go see the real world.

My diet is, you guessed it, pretty boring. Fish, chicken, pork, beef, pasta, rice, vegetables. Lots of spices. Is it something I can trademark and charge a bunch of money for? Again, no. I just eat to live, rather than living to eat. Do I enjoy a good meal? Sure, but what's more important is who I'm eating with rather than what I'm eating. I've been working in my hometown for the past three years, and the most enjoyable meals have been those lunches or dinners I've managed to have with people I've known since high school, not those at the fanciest or most expensive restaurants.

The other person who has called me boring and gotten away with it is my daughter. Just a week or two ago at the dinner table, she said she was glad we have a wonderfully boring family. It turns out that she had an assignment in her American Sign Language class to describe (in sign language) her family. Some of her classmates had to go into great detail about how their dad was on his third marriage and their mom on her second, that they were a child of the second-dad marriage so they have two different sets of half-siblings and other step-siblings, they have half-nieces and nephews, and step-half cousins beyond count. On the other hand, my daughter only had to sign, "One dad, one mom, one brother, and two dogs. And Mom and Dad are married to each other." Again, boring can be good.

How does a marriage last 20 years in this world? And why is that a question? When I was a child, my grandparents and great-grandparents were celebrating 40 or 50 or 60 years, and now that seems so rare. How can you stay attached to the same person you met 25 years ago? Well, that part is less boring, I guess. In fact, it probably causes more elevated blood pressure and heart rates than just about anything else. What it taught me was how important it is to marry well.

MARRY WELL

I realize this idea may be controversial for some, given the current hoopla about same-sex marriage, but it's an important part of my life, and I think it is an important part of anyone's life. I'm in no position to comment on same-sex anything, so I'll just talk about my wife and how we came to be married for over 20 years at this point.

This title sounds pretty arrogant—like I somehow tricked a better person into marrying me. Well, in some ways I feel like I did. I knew for years that I wanted to marry Joselynne; she was the most amazing woman I'd ever met, and I felt I wasn't anywhere near good enough for her. We went to the same high school, but never actually met. My only interaction with her was the morning a friend of mine named Dave came into the cafeteria and said he'd just broken up with his girlfriend the night before. As we talked, I guess she came in the door behind me so he made a comment like, "There's the ***** that dumped me." I turned around, looked at her, and said to Dave, "Smart girl." He chased me around the cafeteria for a while before we had to go to class.

Joselynne was a year behind me in school, so I was in my second year of university when she arrived. We were living in the same residence complex, so we saw each other regularly. On one particular day we ended up elbows deep in a photocopier, trying to get something to print, covered in black toner and laughing hysterically as we destroyed—I mean disassembled—the copier to get at a paper jam deep in its bowels. But although we saw each other a lot, one or the other of us always seemed to be in a relationship.

I resorted to making a wish. She was a volunteer with Big Sisters, and her "little sister" found out my birthday was coming up, so she wanted to bake me a cake. When she put the cake in front of me, she told me to make a wish, and I wished that someday Joselynne would become my wife. Of course, she asked what I wished for, so I had to say, "I can't tell you or it won't come true." Well, four years and two weeks later, my wish came true, but I'm getting ahead of myself. We had a bunch of stuff to learn first.

We had become very close friends, so we decided to share an apartment in my last year of university. That didn't work out so well. We fought—a lot. At Christmas break she moved into her own place, and we saw very little of each other for the rest of the year. I graduated into the "worst recession in 20 years" as it was described, and trying to get a job in the oil industry was nearly impossible. I moved to another city with my at-the-time girlfriend so she could attend a different university, and found a job with a pipeline company that sent me to Fort Nelson, BC. In November. At minus 45 degrees Celsius. It's not quite in the Arctic Circle (66 degrees north latitude) but it's close (about 59 degrees). I went north, my girlfriend stayed in Vancouver, and we eventually broke up. Sometime around February I realized that living up north had certain tax advantages—I could take holidays and the government would let me write off the costs, so I started looking for someplace to go and the Montreal Jazz Festival sounded like a great idea. Joselynne was attending McGill University, so I wrote her a letter. (A letter is a piece of paper that you write on and then put in an envelope...never mind). I said I was coming to the jazz festival and would she like to get together. Well, we wrote back and forth and eventually I got on an airplane to fly to Montreal. I had a room at a Howard Johnson's hotel in downtown Montreal near the festival and it had two beds. This is important because of what happened when I arrived. It seems one of the other tenants in Joselynne's building had moved in bringing along a cockroach infestation, which spread to the rest of the building, and the building was being fumigated the day after I arrived. To this day, my wife accuses me of having something to do with this event, but I maintain my innocence—there are no cockroaches in Fort Nelson, BC. When she told me about the situation, I said there was an extra bed in my hotel room, and since the only alternative for her was staying with her parents who lived a couple of hours outside downtown, she agreed.

As I said, boring is good, so nothing happened. I attended the jazz festival during the days while she did research on her master's degree, and we went to jazz festival events in the evenings. I met some of her friends, we had a wonderful time, and on the night before I left, we had a long talk about whether we should start a relationship. I know; can you believe two people would discuss the topic rather than just jumping into it? Well, believe it or not, we did. We talked about the pros and cons of a cross-country relationship, how my last long-distance relationship didn't work very well, and whether we wanted to ruin our friendship if a relationship didn't work out.

So how did I know she was the right person for me? At the time I probably couldn't have put it into words, but the benefit of 25 plus years to think it over helped me realize there were four things that turned me on about her.

First was intellectual. When we shared the apartment, we would regularly stay up all night talking (yes, kids, just talking) about anything and everything. There were countless nights where the signal we should stop talking was the sound of the newspaper hitting the ground outside the apartment door. We would discuss, debate, and just talk about our thoughts, our feelings, etc. I know it sounds somewhat corny, but I think that's the first key to a long term relationship—you need to feel supported AND stimulated intellectually by the other person.

Second was emotional. I can't really explain why I feel the way I do when I'm around my wife, I just know that I do feel something very strongly. When I'm away from her, I miss her, and when we're close, I feel, I don't know, just "right." Sorry I can't be more specific on this one, but it's just something I feel.

Third was spiritual. I know this one will turn some people off, which is why I used the word spiritual rather than religious. I have my faith, and my wife had a lot to do with it. I'm not saying everyone should have the same as me, but you really do need to have a common understanding of spirituality with your partner. Can a Muslim marry a Catholic, or a Jew marry a Christian? I'm sure they can, and in the seven billion people on the planet I'm sure it's happened countless times. In fact, my faith has changed over the course of my relationship with my wife. Together we have probably come closer to each other's understanding, rather than one person "convincing" the other. If you're in a relationship with someone, it's probably more important that you have similar answers to "Is there a God?" than if you go to the same specific denomination of church.

And fourth, in my opinion, is physical. There really is a physical, animal attraction I have to my wife. And I've felt it since we were in our teens. Does that mean I don't notice the Victoria's Secret ads on TV, or the lady in the car next to me, or whatever other distractions come along? Of course not. The difference it two-fold I guess. First, I have the other three attractions to my wife, and second, I actually meant the vows I spoke when we got married. Does that make me out of touch with the times? Maybe. Maybe those who believe humans aren't supposed to be monogamous are right, and maybe they're wrong. What my life has taught me so far, though, is that it's not about me, it's about my kids. And the only way my kids turned out the way they have is that my wife and I are still married to each other. I'm a widow's son, so I have some experience of living with a single parent. It probably taught me more about gender equality than any class or schooling ever could. I learned my mom could do all the things the other dads were doing—get the car fixed, have a job, etc—plus she was able to take care of my sister and me; and when I was 12 she managed to find another man to fall in love with. They've been married almost 35 years and they're just pathetic about it. I think it's wonderful.

HAVE FAITH

I realize this topic will be touchy for some people, and I understand if you want to skip to the next section, or maybe even the next chapter, but I'd ask you to just consider the point. If you had asked me in my twenties whether I would be regularly attending a church by this time, and even having a leadership position, I'd have thought you were loopy. I didn't believe in anything bigger than myself at that time, but I've come to the conclusion that we as people do need something else. There's a famous theological argument called Pascal's Wager. Basically it says that either God (or whichever Supreme Being) exists, or He doesn't. Nothing a human does or says can change that. On our part, either a human can believe, or not. And whichever one a human chooses has no effect on whether God exists or not (unlike Santa ClausJ).

So, as any good consultant knows, this is the prototypical 2×2 consulting matrix. The outcomes are pretty simple—if He exists and you don't believe, you're in trouble. If He doesn't exist and you don't believe, nothing happens. If He doesn't exist and you do believe, you get a code to live by and maybe a community of fellow believers. If he does exist and you do believe, you get everything (depending on your beliefs). What Pascal said was, if I choose not to believe either I lose everything or I get nothing, but if I choose to believe, either I get everything or I lose nothing. Seems a simple choice.

Even the founder of Alcoholics Anonymous included a "higher power" in his design. Christians say people are born with a "God-shaped hole in our hearts." Whatever you feel about the question, my suggestion is you consider a faith, and have one.

I made my final decision on the side of a road in Orange County about eight years ago. My wife was in the hospital, we didn't know what was wrong, and it wasn't clear that she was going to make it. I had to rush home to get some paperwork and check on my kids, and all of a sudden I just started to cry so hard I couldn't see the road. I pulled over so I didn't crash and it just hit me that I couldn't get through what I was going through on my own. I needed help, and I prayed. If you're expecting me to describe a "road to Damascus" revelation, I'm afraid to disappoint you. I didn't see Jesus, or anyone else for that matter. I just knew that praying helped. Since then my wife and I have attended a church near where we live, and I was asked to serve on a pastor-nominating committee when the senior pastor took a position in another State. Through that experience, I learned more about church internal business than I ever wanted to know, but I also learned a lot about myself and my faith. And what I've gone through in the past few years has made my faith stronger, not weaker. My wife and I volunteer in the nursery at our church two or three Sundays a month, and we try to attend a discussion group as often as we can. Does this make us better than anyone else? Absolutely not. Does it help us ground ourselves and our children in a set of values that we hope helps make the world a better place? We hope so. Our son, a senior in high school, is planning a career in youth ministry and currently struggling with the decision of which college to attend for a degree in religious studies or theology. The empathy he showed that Christmas Eve has continued throughout his life.

SO WHAT

Ok, so it's now the deadline for my submission. Yes, tonight. Once again I'll refrain from suggesting 20-somethings avoid procrastination.

I guess the key points from my story really are what I thought when I started.

Life really isn't about me. According to the actuaries, my life is more than half over. My two children will live for another 70 or 80 years, meaning they will live until nearly the end of the twenty-first century. The target audience for this project has another 60 or 70 years of life, depending on gender and where they live. Think about your own children, your own legacy. What will they do, and who will they become? Worry less about what you own or what you do, but focus on how you raise those children.

Be boring. Get into good habits, go outside, run around, and play with your kids. Let them see your good habits—believe me, they'll notice those much more than what you tell them.

Marry well. Look for that person who stimulates you intellectually, emotionally, spiritually, and physically. Don't settle, but don't run away if you fight (verbally, I mean). You may find that person that drives you nuts really is the person to drive you nuts.

Have faith. There will come a time in your life when you realize you don't want to believe in nothing. Find something to believe in, and learn everything you can about it. Have a code you live by (and not the "Bro Code" from *How I Met Your Mother*, the final episode of which I'm watching as I type this...)

RUSSELL

"We have a FIFO principle when we hire people here," said the large sweating man sitting across the table from me in a crumpled grey suit and blue shirt. His dark grey tie was loosened and the top button of his shirt undone, revealing folds on his thick neck. He took off his glasses and wiped them on his shirt, grinned at me and looked at me with his puffy grey eyes, enjoying his power over this young eager new recruit. "Fit in or F-Off!" he added, looking rather pleased with himself with what he thought was a very clever accounting pun referring to the FIFO (first-in-first-out) accounting principle for inventory.

I was 21 years old and interviewing for a job as an articled clerk with Price Waterhouse. This Chartered Accountant (CA) was the "esteemed" partner who was to be my mentor and exemplar in the integrity, principles, ethics and morals of the CA profession. "Fit in or F-Off!"?? Being innocent and fairly naive for my age, I didn't quite know what to make of his comment, but was happy nonetheless when he offered me the job and the opportunity to article under his supervision. Little did I know that his comment would become a theme for the next 25 years of my life and my career as I struggled to fit in with a culture where I did not belong, both at work and in the country where I was born and raised.

I was born in Pretoria, South Africa to Richard and Raye Cullingworth. I guess I was lucky to be the youngest of five children, and benefitted from the lessons my parents learnt and wisdom they gained raising the other four. At each stage of my life, they had experienced parenting four other children through the same stages of life, so for me it was a breeze. Mostly I think they had learnt to relax in their parenting and I was a very compliant child who wanted to please them, so our relationship was very positive and cooperative, even as a teenager. I also think I was fortunate to inherit some of the best traits of each of them—from my dad, it was his curiosity and intellect, and from my mom it was her sensitivity, softness and love and care for people.

During my teenage years, I developed a love for music, drama, surfing and art. I would much rather be at drama practice or at home sketching caricatures than be doing my homework or studying for an exam. My academic schoolwork suffered from my involvement in the band, choir, surfing, field hockey and lead roles in school plays. Looking back now though, I wouldn't change a thing because I was developing a well-rounded, broad sphere of interest that would become one of my strengths and serve me well as an adult. I was very proud of my acting and embraced it with everything I had. In my final year of school, I played the lead role of King Arthur in the musical, *Camelot*—a demanding role for a 17-year-old in a three-hour-long play. I immersed myself in this role and loved every minute of it.

DRAFTED

Academically I was typically above average, but struggled with two subjects in particular: accounting, which I failed in Grade 10, and mathematics, which I failed to pass in Grade 12. In the South African school system, we were required to pass two subjects on a "higher grade" level in order to gain entrance to university. My two higher grade subjects were geography and mathematics, but with a failing grade in mathematics I was unable to enter university. My only alternative to university was to report to the South African Defense Force for my two-year compulsory conscription.

In South Africa at the time, every white South African male

was conscripted into the South African Defence Force. It was 1985 and the country was at the tail end of the 13-year war with Angola over what was then South West Africa, now Namibia. I was assigned to the South African Medical (SAMED) Forces to be trained as an army medic. At the tender age of 17 I boarded a train at midnight into my two-year "sentence" for being white and young and South African. I didn't support the government, the Angola war or the racist propaganda that I had been subjected to my whole life. Boot camp (called Basic Training Camp) was a three-month-long nightmare but it shook the mommy's boy out of me and taught me one of my most important lessons in life—to suck it up and not let anyone or my circumstances get me down.

Mostly I got into trouble for being unable to hide my big grin and finding everything quite funny. I got to know "die boom" (the tree) very well, which was exactly one kilometer away from our barracks and I was sent back and forth to wipe the smile off my face. Our Afrikaans corporal would direct his hand to the tree and say, "Cullingworth, sien jy die boom? Daar gat jy!" (Cullingworth, do you see the tree? Off you go!) Boot camp was serious business. I had two platoon mates who tried to commit suicide to escape their circumstances. Others were badly bullied; some sustained injuries.

We had bush warfare drills in the stifling upper 35-degree Celsius heat of the South African interior. I remember during one such drill, we had to run through the bush and then dive into cover on hearing the corporal's whistle, and then crawl, walk in a crouched position or run depending on sequential whistle signals (like a well-trained dog). It was a very hot afternoon. I heard the command and dived into some long grass, landing next to a deep muddy pit. Without thinking, I slid into the mud with all my clothes and gear, and remember how great the cool water felt against my skin and not worrying about being covered in mud. I think it is valuable once in a while to be in a situation where you realize what really matters and then the inconsequential little issues in life just fade away.

After boot camp I was transferred to my home town of East London, where I worked in the pharmacy at the army medical depot and volunteered on weekends at the emergency ward, stitching up knife and machete wounds and assisting the doctors with more complex facial stitching and working on deeper stab wounds and cuts. I managed this very well and actually found it very interesting. There is still a part of me that believes and wishes that I could have been a doctor, but my better-than-average-but-less-than-stellar academic grades in high school prevented me from entering any medical program. I was too late to learn an important life lesson for students—work hard at school or university because excellent grades give you the option to choose any program you want.

Something significant happened while I was in the army. I mentioned before that I had failed higher grade mathematics in grade 12 and as such did not qualify for university entrance. I was given permission to write a make-up exam, but the date of the exam was in the middle of my basic training, so studying was out of the question. I was given a three-day weekend pass in order to write the exam, but instead of studying over the weekend, I spent time with my family and friends and didn't open a book. As a result I received my lowest grade ever. If you think an "F" is bad, I received an "H"(0%-20%). I believed I could still pass if I put my mind to it, and in my second year of army I re-did the entire year's math curriculum on my own, in my spare time, and at the end of the year, in December, I wrote and passed the higher grade exam.

SWIMMING UPSTREAM

Now what? I could enter university, but what did I want to study? In making this very important decision, I made a critical, life changing, misjudgement. I didn't know myself well enough, or know enough to take the time to analyze and think about who I was at my core, and what I enjoyed. I relied on those who I thought knew me best to tell me what I should do, and I think the advice, while well intentioned, had more to do with the wishes and experience of my advisors than with me and who I was. My oldest brother was a chartered accountant and my dad had a lot of admiration for accounting as a career choice. I remember my dad's words as he advised me, "Well, if you don't like it you can always go and do something else, but you will always have a solid financial foundation." He was right about the solid financial foundation part, but totally wrong about simply going to do something else.

Under this advice, and in the absence of any better ideas, I enrolled in the Bachelor of Accounting Science program at the University of South Africa. Being the fifth child of a minister, there was no university fund to pay my way, so my only choice was to do my degree through distance education while I worked through my articles of clerkship with Price Waterhouse. Working while studying was fairly common amongst articled clerks, so the culture of hard work kept me going—no partying and messing around at night. I despised the dull work and the course materials, especially auditing and corporate law, and that should have been my first clue, but I had been raised to suck up my complaints, be disciplined and work hard to succeed. In the early stages of my career I was lucky to have an excellent middle manager, Tony, who mentored me and taught me the discipline and focus needed to succeed in accounting, but everything about the profession was an awkward fit for me and I felt like I was constantly swimming upstream, struggling in a career where success depended on excelling in my weaknesses.

At this early and impressionable age though, I remember watching the two partners at our Price Waterhouse office drink themselves into a stupor at corporate retreats, and I noticed every time they bent the rules, lied and cheated. This was a dilemma for me, and I couldn't understand the disparity between the "high ethical standards of the profession" that I was learning about in my classes and the reality of how unethical and unprofessional the partners were at my firm.

My principal partner made another classic comment that stuck with me for the rest of my life. I was at a more senior stage now, being in my fourth year of articles. He sat me down in the boardroom for my annual evaluation, with the other, quieter and more placid partner sitting next to him, and although his feedback was generally positive regarding my work, he had some negative feedback about my personality. "You are too friendly with the clients," he said. "We want them to like us, not to love us." At this early age, despite being vastly his junior in the firm and in the industry, I knew he was wrong. "I don't agree," I said nervously. "If our clients don't love us, they will walk with the next firm that offers them a lower rate for their audit," I said. Contradicting a partner was a career-limiting move for sure and he wasn't at all happy with me.

It took me another 20 years to understand what was happening here. As a friendly, popular, energetic, funny, extraverted and engaging people-person, I was a misfit in the accounting profession and my behaviours were standing out as "wrong" to those around me. I didn't understand. Neither did they. This would become the theme of my accounting career, and ultimately cause me to change jobs after two to three years like clockwork.

Another important decision I made while working at Price Waterhouse was getting married at the young age of 23, against the advice of others around me. I look back now and wonder what I was thinking. I didn't know who I was, but I thought I knew who I wanted to be. I thought I wanted to be a family man, settled down with kids. I felt I wanted to rescue her and create a better life for her. I didn't think too much about it. My wife and I had a difficult relationship from the very first week after our honeymoon, with the shock of living with each other for the first time. Despite our differences, we made the most of the good times and our first daughter, Grace, was born when I was only 25 years old.

I had graduated with my Bachelor of Accounting and Auditing

degree and completed my prerequisite five years articles of clerkship, and was still working at Price Waterhouse and studying part-time to complete my honours degree in accounting, a prerequisite for a South African CA designation. If I hated the course material in my undergrad, then I absolutely loathed the content of the honours degree even more—no disrespect to those who love the complexities of triple consolidations, mergers and acquisitions, but this was the death of my accounting studies. I dropped out of the honours program and decided to leave public practice and to try working as a consultant or commercial accountant.

"You will never be a CA!" retorted the enraged Price Waterhouse partner when I handed him my resignation. As it turned out, he would be absolutely correct, and that would be one of the better decisions I had made in my life.

CANADA

I worked as a commercial accountant in South Africa until 1995, when my wife and I applied to immigrate to Canada. With increased crime and rapidly declining quality of education, South Africa was becoming a bit too unsafe for us. By now we had two daughters, Grace and Paige, and South Africa did not feel like a safe place to raise them. I had six friends who had been murdered, including the elderly photographer at our wedding and his wife, our pharmacist and my best friend's grandfather, who was murdered during a robbery of his little Chinese corner store. My brother had been shot in the leg in his driveway when thieves tried to steal his car.

As a father and husband, I had very little peace of mind, scouting my driveway before getting out of the car and locking everything up, including ourselves, behind steel bars and security gates. I worried at night about protecting my family if we were burgled or possibly held at gunpoint in our own home. This was no way to live and I determined that it would be best to live in a country where we were safe and, more importantly, where my daughters could flourish.

In 1995 we applied as skilled immigrants to Canada and in January 1996 we received our Landed Immigrant Visas from the Canadian Embassy. With much enthusiasm, hope and optimism, we planned everything very carefully, sold our house and everything we didn't want to take with us, shipped our container over and then boarded a plane for Vancouver via Singapore in July 1996. Little did I know how much Canada would change my life.

My Canadian experience was exciting and challenging. I had to unlearn some of the South African cultural behaviours that are not accepted in Canadian culture and the Canadian workplace. South Africans are very direct and typically say exactly what is on their mind, even if it may sound rude or offensive, which is generally accepted in the culture. I have found that many Canadians appreciate (a toned-down version of) South African directness and quirky humour in personal and social circles, but there is not much appreciation in the workplace, where politeness, niceness and social grace and acceptable behaviours are the norm. Unfortunately, these are accompanied by less desirable behaviours like conflict avoidance, false harmony, passive resistance, stubbornness and rumour. I had to learn the hard way. I would later come to understand that these are the stereotypical good- and bad-day traits of an introverted feeling culture, and that the white South African culture was the opposite, an extraverted thinking culture.

After five weeks of looking for work, I was hired as controller for a small engineering company with 14 employees. It was difficult for me to accept being "managed" by someone with no qualifications and absolutely no people skills, but I considered myself lucky; many immigrants make much greater sacrifices in order to get local work experience. While working at this small company I was very fortunate to be accepted into the Simon Fraser University (SFU) Executive MBA program. I had only been in Canada a year but had managed to score in the top 20% in North America on the GMAT exam, which helped me to gain a seat in the SFU Program. Entering the Executive MBA was exciting and challenging and required me to take a large student loan which I could hardly afford, but I knew that this investment would pay itself back many times over. What I didn't know was the extent to which this education would change my life, from the inside out, and push my personal and professional life into directions which I could never imagine.

My first benefit of being in the MBA program was a career change. I was hired by the Certified General Accountants Association of Canada (CGA-Canada) as manager of business planning and was later promoted to controller. Through my MBA I had not only learnt the skills and techniques for business, I had learnt something profound—to trust myself and my decision-making ability, to be confident, to manage risk and to believe that I had a great set of internal skills and values. This not only changed my behaviour at work, but in my personal life too. In coming to Canada my undergrad degree meant nothing, my experience meant very little. I understood this, because how is any hiring manager supposed to know the difference in quality between the universities in the world, and all the immigrants who arrive in BC with degrees and experience from other countries? Who is to say which is better, or worse, or equivalent to Canadian standards? Once I had achieved a Canadian standard of education, employers were comfortable and knowledgeable about what that meant in terms of standards of education, and so I became a more highly valued commodity. This helped tremendously with my confidence and self-esteem. I walked differently, dressed differently and talked confidently—well worth the cost of admission.

This inner confidence changed my marriage relationship. No longer was I the agreeable, mild-mannered and eager-to-please young guy that would do anything for his wife and not stand up for himself. My newfound assertiveness and need for purpose changed our relationship to the point that would ultimately lead to separation and divorce. Not an ideal choice by any means, and one that should be avoided until it is an absolute last resort. My wife and I had agreed to try to stay together until our daughters had finished school, but we never made it that far. My MBA was the beginning of the end of our marriage (MBA is often jokingly referred to as Marriages Break Apart).

I stayed at CGA-Canada for almost three years, but again, struggled to fit in with the accounting culture. The president took me for lunch and repeated what had become a familiar theme: my work was excellent but my personality was a problem, and unless I was willing to change to fit in, it was not going to work out well for me. I resigned the following day.

FOLLOW THE ENERGY PATH

Another epiphany happened to change my working life and my outlook on work. I was pondering the scientific law on the conservation of energy that says "energy cannot be created or destroyed, only converted from one form to another." I thought about myself, and my energy. I am a machine, and I eat food for energy, which is converted into another form every day in my work and play, burning up my energy (mental and physical) and wearing out my brain and my body every day until I die. For example, a craftsman's energy is added to a pile of wood and converted into a beautiful piece of furniture, a nurse's energy is converted into physical and emotional healing in others.

I puzzled over the question: If I follow the path of my energy conversion at work, into what is my energy being converted? In my mind I followed my "energy path" and at the end was a disappointing and disillusioning result. Throughout my career, my energy had been transformed into a meaningless outcome—money in the bank account of someone who was already vastly wealthier than I would ever be. This realization was extremely powerful and would change my working life forever.

REVELATION

In 2006 I was very fortunate to be appointed as director of finance at Canuck Place Children's Hospice, a wonderful, loving and caring organization described as "a place between heaven and earth." Working at Canuck Place was a wonderful experience; the Canuck Place team are incredible and wonderful people. I relished the opportunity to get involved with the work and to get to know some of the children and families, but ran into a roadblock in the form of my boss, the CEO, who expressed that it was not the place of the director of finance to get involved with the work or the families. This became a sticking point between us as time wore on, despite the fact that I had stipulated at the interview that I did not want to be relegated to the back office "doing the books." On one occasion, in a moment of frustration with my desire to get involved, the CEO exclaimed, "I don't know what to do with you Russell. You should become a counsellor or something!" Again, in a moment of exasperation with me, my boss had expressed a truth that had been there all along. I knew that she was absolutely correct.

It was at Canuck Place that I received my greatest life-changing revelation. The executive team had been donated an "Insights Discovery Development Session" by a generous corporate donor. While I had received psychological profiles before, nothing could compare to the Insights Discovery Personal Profile I received as foundation to this training session.

The difference was that the Insights Program revealed our two personas: who we are instinctively (less conscious persona) compared to the face we wear—the person we believe we "should be" (our conscious persona). This clearly revealed to me that I had been trying to play the role of accountant—I had learned the skills and behaviours—yet my instinctive and more authentic self was exactly the opposite. Through my 25-year career, from Price Waterhouse to Canuck Place, my bosses and I had wrestled and disagreed over my personality, not the quality of my work. I showed up in a way that was contradictory to how accountants should show up, and that was a dichotomy and unacceptable in almost every job I held. Society has expectations of how accountants should behave, yet I never fit those expectations, and that was a big problem. During that Insights Discovery session, I secretly vowed that I would leave the accounting profession and find a way to work with my natural strengths and passions, work with people and, even better, be able to share, teach and present.

The most powerful impression during that day of revelation was a deep wish that someone would have taught me more about myself when I was in my twenties. This would have saved me so much time, confusion, job-hopping and heartbreak. I certainly would not have chosen accounting as a career. Recognizing the depth of our differences, I would probably not have married my "opposite type." As I contemplated this, a dream and concept took shape.

In May 2010 I left Canuck Place and in July 2010 I founded the Centre of Excellence for Young Adults (CEYA). I was fortunate enough to be accepted for accreditation by Insights Vancouver as an Insights Discovery Licensed Practitioner. My research led me into the field of Emotional Intelligence (EQ) and I quickly realized that Insights Discovery is really about developing EQ. As I learned more, I came to believe that Emotional Intelligence is THE MOST IMPORTANT SKILL I could ever learn. The competencies of EQ are self-awareness, self-management, social awareness and social management, with self-awareness being the foundational competency but no more important than the others. I founded EQAdvantage Learning and Development to provide Insights Training to companies, and EQinLove.com to provide advice on how EQ competencies can help relationships to thrive.

Personally, I have come to believe that EQ will ultimately lead to wisdom, knowledge and understanding, which is about other people, not about intellect, money, power or material wealth. I have come to learn and believe that true happiness and fulfillment in life, Maslow's "Self Actualization" at the top of his hierarchy of needs, come from a greater sense of community and giving of self (my energy) to others without an expectation of return. Many rich business people would hate the business model, but then again, they may not be internally happy and fulfilled people. My guess is that they will keep searching until they find out that true wealth has very little to do with money. These are the lessons I have learnt in life, and I believe that, regardless of my material wealth, I live, and will continue to live a very happy and fulfilled life.

"They deem me mad because I will not sell my days for gold; and I deem them mad because they think my days have a price."

Khalil Gibran

SANDIE

I grew up in a protected household where the world was either black or white; there were no shades of grey to colour decisions or actions. As a result, I did not use my teens to explore who I was and make mistakes. I had to wait until I was on my own at the age of 20. I then proceeded to make many mistakes in my early twenties, some of which would have lasting consequences.

At the age of 20, I planned a year away from university (in Ontario, Canada) to travel around Australia, where I had been born. I had a keen desire to learn more about my past and to understand where my life had taken root. At the time, I made the difficult decision to leave behind someone I felt was my soul mate. It was made more challenging by the fact that he didn't feel the same, which aggravated my already low sense of self-esteem and self-confidence.

FEAR AND PRIDE

My experience in Australia actually didn't do anything to improve my self-confidence or to help me gain an understanding of myself. I met many selfish, critical and negative people, and rather than take that as a signal to move on, I travelled with them in my youthful desire to belong to a group. Looking back, I think it was fear throughout my twenties and even into my thirties that kept me grounded in one place, rather than having the courage to move on.

I have to be honest and say that my fear was mixed with a good dose of pride. In my twenties, I was often trying to take on the world and prove something—anything—to myself, to my friends and to my family. I got caught up in the desire to seek approval, and took very little time to understand myself. I was listening to the voices in my head telling me what I should do—what the perception was of where I was living, what relationship I was in, what fabulous job I had—rather than what was it that I really wanted to be and with whom.

MOVING, BUT IN THE WRONG DIRECTION

Fear and pride are a potent "cocktail" when you're young. But mix in the need to prove to the world that you're always making progress and the road you pave will be full of potholes, and you'll make wrong turns.

Growing up, my family didn't sit still. We were always in motion. Even if you were going in the wrong direction, you kept moving. Motion was viewed positively, while pausing was viewed as idleness. Looking back, I wish I had given myself permission and overcome my fear of a perceived failure to pause and to consider all my options in terms of education, career, relationships and more importantly who I was. I would've benefited greatly from examining my life and using that time in a valuable way by asking for professional help, as well as the advice of close friends. Instead, I barrelled full steam ahead—and often in the wrong direction.

Consciously choosing to pause, particularly in your twenties when you're ambitious and have the energy to save the world, means having confidence in your inner voice, and more importantly, listening to what it tells you. It takes courage to avoid "helpful" advice from others who often mean well, but may be letting their own fears shape their advice. It takes courage to pause, listen to yourself and to follow your own path.

LEARNING THE HARD WAY

It took me until my forties to understand how to tune in and trust my instincts. Once I started to do that, I made better decisions because I was pausing and listening to myself.

That's a huge lesson. Running away, avoiding a situation, conversation or person may ease pain, loneliness or discomfort in the short term. But until you address your issues, and your feelings you will be unable to grow into your true self.

I learned the hard way. I didn't ask for help. I didn't seek support. I let fear and pride assert their power over my inner voice and confidence. I kept moving without considering the direction and I allowed my early conditioning to define my approach to life.

My turning point came when I joined a professional organization in my late twenties. In this environment, I was encouraged to do many things that I hadn't given myself permission to consider all through my twenties. I took time to consider options, seek the support and collaboration of colleagues, and develop plans to achieve goals aligned with our expectations. The nurturing environment encouraged positive thinking, team spirit and it allowed me to be vulnerable so I could learn and grow.

While I was applying these lessons in my professional life, the progression was slower in my personal life. My husband and I were raising three young children and all our energy and focus was dedicated to them. Neglecting yourself and the person you are most intimate with will take a toll spiritually, emotionally and physically. I have firsthand experience.

YOU DON'T NEED TO HIT ROCK BOTTOM TO ASK FOR HELP

Gabor Mate, M.D., a Vancouver-based doctor, is an international expert on the direct link between emotional stress and physical illness such as auto-immune diseases and some types of cancer. At the age of 42, having three children aged ten, eight and five, juggling their activities, my personal fitness and a 30-hour-a-week job, the physical stress coupled with the emotional turmoil of an unfulfilling marriage took its toll. I suffered complete cortisol and adrenal failure.

A wise person once told me that you don't need to hit rock bottom to ask for help. Unfortunately for me, I let that happen and the climb out of the hole was steep. But through counselling and supportive family and friends, I finally took the time to discover who I was, what I would accept in my life, and recognize the negativity I didn't want in my life.

But 20 years is a very long time to be uncertain or unhappy with whom you are, or to not understand and appreciate who you are. If you learn anything from my experience, I hope you take away a couple of lessons.

First, **take time to listen to your inner self and get comfortable with who you are**. This isn't easy at 20, but it's important that you start to tune into your inner voice.

Secondly, you also need to know **its ok to ask for help**. Reaching out isn't a sign of weakness. It's reflective of our human spirit that seeks to connect.

I know that as I enter the next phase of my life, I will continue to change. But having learned the hard lessons of my life, I know that my internal barometer—who I am, what I feel, what I believe—will not. You need to remember that your internal barometer will keep you steady as you navigate life. And while it may be dented by circumstances and situations outside of your control, it will be your inner self that you come back to.

Now in my late forties, I couldn't be happier. I am confident in who I am as an individual. I recognize my weaknesses, but I am more focused on my strengths and the things that fill me with self-respect, peace and contentment, and therefore, happiness. My husband and I have put our relationship with God first, one another next, and then our role as parents. We have a respectful and kind relationship and are better role models and parents to our children as a result. Our children continue to bring us much joy. For me, having children was the best single decision my husband and I have ever made, and I can't imagine my life without each of them.

MOVING FORWARD

One of the best pieces of advice **Maya Angelou** ever gave was this: *"I've learned that you shouldn't go through life with a catcher's mitt on both hands; you need to be able to throw something back."*

Best wishes on finding yourself, being yourself and enjoying yourself. Throw everything back that doesn't fill you with self-respect and love.

SÉBASTIEN

What an interesting topic to give advice to future generations, especially for someone who is still trying to find his way, or to be more precise, someone who gets easily bored in a comfort zone. After all, life is only interesting when you set up new challenges for yourself and when you have objectives. If your only motive is to wait for the end, then you don't need to do anything to reach it successfully.

ABOUT CHOICES

For me, life is about the choices you make, starting from childhood. I remember the first choice that I was given when I was around six years old and I had to decide what sport to practice. At that age you just want to do what the majority does, which often leads to the worst choice; and, thus, I went for football (soccer). After just four hours I decided that it definitely wasn't for me. Thinking about it 30 years after, I realize that it was the first of a long line of experiences that taught me that acting as others did was always the best recipe to make the wrong choice.

After football, I tried swimming, athletics, basketball, handball, skateboard, BMX and mountain biking. Biking brought me two things: first, I was feeling better in an individualist sport where your ranking depends only on your direct performance; and secondly, I was feeling better in the mountains than practicing sport in cities in the middle of the crowd. This is probably what brought me to high mountain climbing, where the higher you get the quieter and most beautiful is the landscape, especially above 3,500 metres.

Another big choice I had to make, and that many people face also, is to choose a university and the topic of study. On that I was happy with only 50 percent of my choice. To choose the topic, I followed the French system that pushes you to do engineering when you are good at math. That was the choice I regretted, mainly because it wasn't fully my own choice, so of course it was going to have consequences that did not align with me.

The second half was to choose the university. I wanted to go to Ireland to learn English, to discover new latitudes and meet new people. As my level of English was terrible, the school refused to write me a recommendation letter to send me over there. The trigger point was when they told me, "We cannot help you to enroll in an Irish university because you will fail." So, instead I went to Ireland with no English. I learned the language in three months, then enrolled into Trinity College Dublin and obtained my BSc Eng. with Honors.

If I had accepted the postulate that if you are bad at English at school you can't learn it, then I would have never had the internal force to fight the system and show them that their principle was completely wrong. And without this knowledge of English it would have been much more difficult for me to do my MBA ten years after. I will discuss this point later, but the key is to listen to yourself to be happy, and don't always follow others' advice.

OVERCOME BARRIERS

The most difficult choice I have faced in my life was one year ago when I had the opportunity to move to Colombia. I lived most of my life in the French Alps, was well established and had a peaceful social life; it would have been easy to continue this. The implication of going to Colombia was unknown; I had only spent two months in the country prior to my move and had no Spanish at all. However, this was not a major barrier as I managed to learn English in three months and I thought that to learn Spanish would be fast also.

So what could be the rational reason for a human being to abandon all roots and stability to jump into the big unknown? The key point for me is that I prefer to feel remorse than regret. In other words, it's better to regret something you did than regret not doing it. I knew what would be lost, but had no idea of what would be gained. This is often the case in high-risk situations. Thanks to my experience in stock trading I have become less risk averse and, more important, I'm able to evaluate potential gain associated to a risk and decide quickly if I accept this risk.

DEPENDENCIES

This decision process was long and, as usual, was influenced by internal and external factors, each one influencing the other. The internal factors: I needed change; I was not happy in my situation; I wanted to be fully independent. The external factors: it was getting difficult to get new customers; growth in France and the Eurozone was low; the population in Europe is aging because of the baby boomer generation and thus we are getting more and more into a conservative system. The last external factor: I had an opportunity to sell a procurement company that I had established in Singapore.

The thing that helped me decide to move was that I didn't want to be dependent on any kind of boss for my work. When you are an employee you depend on your boss. When you are independent you are tied to your customers or shareholders or to the bank; so it doesn't matter where you work, your work is always driven by external factors. This is the main reason why I started doing a trading technique called scalping; it gives me the freedom to work when I want. Plus, when scalping, as you are in position in the market for one to five minutes, you have an immediate feedback and evaluation of your work and this evaluation is completely objective; either you increase or decrease your capital.

Trading is my passion because it gives me total freedom. It requires that you understand your environment and your own psychological way of acting; it teaches you to think and learn by yourself, gives you immediate feedback on your performance, and allows you to set your own objectives and schedule. In my opinion, it is the best school of life because you interact every day with the whole world, and it makes you foresee people's reactions to the market.

So my work as a trader helped me choose moving to Colombia, because I wasn't dependent on a specific geographical position to practice my job, or to any stakeholders.

DON'T FOLLOW ADVICE

My main and most valuable recommendation would be to not follow advice. Of course, such a statement has to be taken into consideration with reflection. The key point is to think for yourself, i.e., listen to a broad variety of people with different backgrounds and then build your own mindset out of this. Whatever advice is given to you, it can't be strictly applied because of differences of education and culture.

The past builds the future and, thus, depending on one's background, it is not always feasible to act in the most rational way possible or at least on a chosen path. The key thing is that you should be able to discern for yourself what advice is good and what is bad, and which advice can be applied to a given situation, depending on your own style, feelings, emotions, values.

Another important point about taking advice from others is to know why their advice is pertinent. It is easy to think that if someone has been successful in his or her life then by following that person's thoughts you should manage to be as prosperous. Many people have read Warren Buffet books, but not many people are good traders. Many people have a dozen books by great chefs in their library, but after having eaten at many relatives' places I can tell you that you don't become a chef by reading books.

This brings us to three major points:

How to define a good professional

There are consensuses that say that you need to be recognized by your peers. This can be easily proved. A good chef is not the one whose restaurant is full every day; being popular is not necessarily being good. A restaurant can be popular because of its geographical position, trendy locations, prices, or be fashionable because some celebrities went there. However, to have three stars in the Michelin Guide has nothing to do with having a waiting line in front of your restaurant, but is related to the quality of the food, service and atmosphere as judged by experts, not by the crowd.

How to define a successful person

Some people would say having a big house, big car, big swimming pool, big bank statement, big Jacuzzi and big belly defines success. Others would say that transmitting knowledge or educating future generations is a quality of success, or that to be successful you need to win a Nobel Prize. Again we are back to our background, education, values, and sometimes dreams, or perhaps the perception we have of ourselves through the views of others. How many of you have done something to try to look good to someone else? We live in a society and most of our choices are influenced by this society and not by our own will. Furthermore, external factors influence the subconscious and, thus, what you think is your own decision can be driven purely by external factors. You need to choose and act before being able to see if it was the right decision for you. You determine if you are a successful person or not.

Without your own experience, advice is useless

You can read as many cookbooks as you wish, nevertheless, without experimenting you will never manage a béchamel sauce or a puff pastry perfectly on the first attempt. The same things occur with trading. Every month I face people who, after reading trading books and having done a bit of back testing and perhaps been lucky on a few real or paper trades, are ruined in 24 hours. To trade badly or to gamble on financial markets can have serious repercussions.

One of the reasons for failing is that most people tend to try the laziest way, or at least one that seems easy, before reflecting on the topic. Funnily enough, most of the time the laziest way is not the easiest, but because of our psychological bias and lack of experience, we almost never do anything perfectly at first attempt.

Another reason for failure is that it's difficult for human beings to accept error. For example, many compulsive gamblers end up ruined because they don't accept their losses, and they try to recover by betting double. Most traders who go bankrupt face the same situation. They may make one or two mistakes during the day or week. The wise one will turn off his trading platform, think about his mistake and come back stronger the next day. The one who can't cope with this feeling will take a new position with higher risk for his money management and thus out of his trading plan; by then he is not trading anymore, but gambling.

I suggest keeping a logbook on your major decisions to be able to come back to it and analyze afterwards. The logbook can contain topics such as:

- What was the given problem/situation?
- Why did I make that decision?
- What was my state of mind?
- What were the internal factors?
- What were the external factors?

- What were the different options?
- What were the main objectives?

Then you can come back to your logbook and reflect on:

- Did I reach my objectives?
- What was the impact of my actions?
- Did I select the best option given my knowledge at that time?
- How could I have improved my decision process?
- What are the biases I should be aware of in future processes?
- What option didn't I explore at that time? More importantly, why?
- Did I improve as a person by making that decision?
- Do I regret making that decision? Why?

One of the best things I read was, "Do the job you like and you will never need to work again." When I was young I wanted to drive space shuttles into space; now I'm trading Dow Jones, ASX 200, DAX, providing digital consultancy services during the week and administrating a farm on weekends. The gap is huge, but I am happy.

My topic is how to make the right decision, but the issue is what is the purpose of deciding and how do those decisions drive our future. Deciding is difficult because to choose is to renounce something. Choosing the blue bike means no white, yellow or purple bike. Life is a trade-off, where we always need to give up on one side to reach the other one.

Studies show that most people in western culture were happier 30 years ago, and the main reason given is that we had less choice. Thanks to marketing and segmentation, there are myriad products that have the same functionality; for example, choose a mouse for your computer or a pair of running shoes or a pair of skis and you will understand what segmentation is. One could say that it's great to have so much choice, which is true. But the drawback is how long it takes you to choose. The point is that by picking up one product we renounce thousands of others, which leaves us with a feeling of doubt that we are making the right decision.

This brings us to the last topic I would like to talk about, which Leibniz explained well in *Discourse on Metaphysics* and is well summarized in one of his famous quotes:

> Every present state of a simple substance is the natural consequence of its preceding state, in such a way that its present is big with its future.
>
> —*Gottfried Wilhelm von Leibniz (1646–1716)*

The most difficult thing to evaluate when making decisions is to know what gates they will open and what others will close, and the cascade reactions they will imply. You can take as much advice as possible to build your mind and choose the right process, but you will never be able to replicate anyone's path by following their example because of simple cultural or psychological differences. It implies that to a given situation you will not react exactly as someone else. It's usually the slight imperceptible differences that you are not aware of that make the big gap on the final result. So at one stage you need to decide to be a spectator of your own life or to take action and risk managing it.

Life is a bridge between birth and death, so don't be afraid to take risks and learn as much as you can to be able to build a bridge that will look like you expected when you look back. To guide you in your decision-making process and to help you fulfill your own expectations, I give you a schematic on the next page. If you don't follow the crowd and think out of the box (which I hope) and thus read book chapters by the end, don't waste time reading about my life; take this diagram, reflect on it and you will save time. If you do so, you can take advantage of the time saved to make something useful of your life.

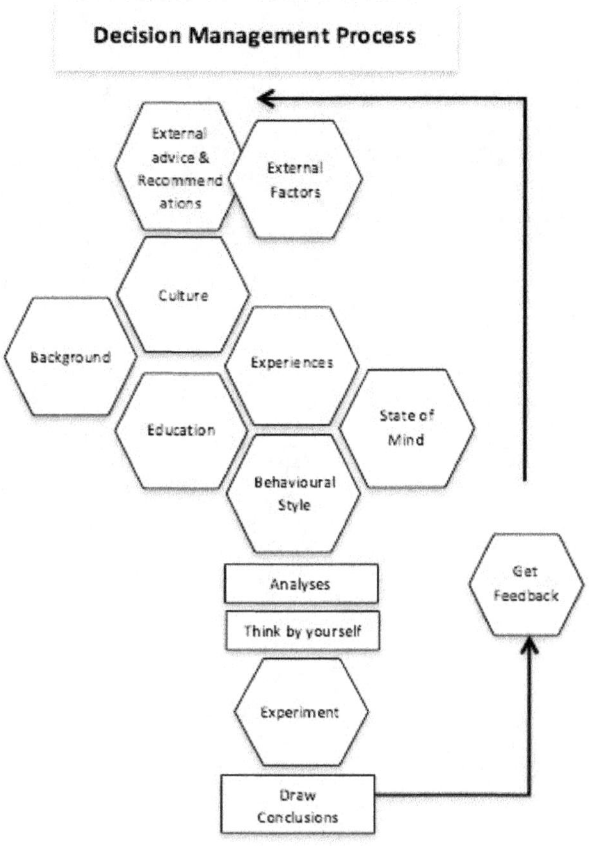

SHANNON

When someone is born, it is my belief that they already have their personalities. I was born an artist. My mother always said that I sang before I started to talk. My parents and older brother are scientists who are talented artistically in their own ways; I ended up being "artsy"—blessed to have their support, but not always understood. For me, it is not just performing. Being an artist is at the core of who I am.

I was born in Canada and raised by Trinidadian parents, and when I was an infant we moved to an American compound in eastern Saudi Arabia. Living in the Middle East enabled my family to travel extensively and I fell in love with traveling. However, I was also dealing with an identity crisis: which country, culturally, I was supposed to identify with?

It was an ongoing struggle to find my place in the world. When I was younger, it was a non-stop battle to fit in; I was racially bullied in elementary and junior high school, and as a young adult I didn't fit the mold at the all-girls boarding school that I attended. So, I kept changing my "persona" on a regular basis. It took me a long time to feel comfortable in my own skin and actually love myself. It took even longer for my purpose in life to be revealed to me. The turning point in my journey happened when I was 20 years old on a trip to Europe. Traveling, pursuing an education, being grateful, praying to God, have made me who I am today, and I know now that I am meant to share through my art with the rest of the world.

IT ALL STARTED IN PARIS

Traveling has always been an integral part of my personal identity. I love meeting people and speaking different languages. After a rough high school experience, I went to Paris for a transition year, living on my own while attending La Sorbonne, the French Studies Department of the University of Paris. Living in Paris as a student at 19 was a dream come true. The rich and varied culture, the arts scene, fashion, architecture, cuisine, nightlife and bohemian spirit appealed to me in a way that no other city had. I sang musical theatre repertoire on the street as a busker for supplemental income, entertained the crowds and loved every minute of it. However, even though my year in Paris was supposed to help me heal, I burnt myself out there in a different way. I partied every night until the wee hours of the morning, trying to forget everything by dancing the night away. I also discovered that my biggest problem is being too trusting. I realized that I wasn't actually the sun and moon to every guy who talked to me, and that I couldn't keep letting my "sometimes" friends crash at my place, especially when they never returned the favor. This experience really pushed me into becoming an adult.

As my year in Paris was coming to a close and I had to return to real life in Canada to finish my university degree, I wanted to soak in every last bit of Europe that I could afford to see. I had this awful fear that I might never get the chance to do it again, and I knew that I hadn't really faced my demons to find ways of coping with my past and find my confidence. So, at 20, I set out on my journey of self-discovery which forever shaped who I am today.

DON'T TAKE LIFE FOR GRANTED

To facilitate my journey, I bought a Eurail pass and paid extra to go to England, as I really wanted to see Stonehenge, Bath, and the White Cliffs of Dover. It was worth it just to look out over those amazing chalky white cliffs to the sea below. I was in awe of the beauty of the Earth and I felt connected with nature in a way that I had forgotten on the paved streets of Paris. On the top of those unique cliffs, spellbound by the phenomenal view, I felt like I was standing on the edge of the world and I could do anything.

I next took off for Bath to see the influences of the Roman baths on that English town, and to see the famous fire blown glass being made. While there, I saw an outdoor performance of my favourite playwright, Shakespeare's *The Tempest*, and I was in heaven. The night I left Bath on my way to Stonehenge via Canterbury, I took the train overnight with a Japanese girl and five guys from Spain, France, Portugal, and Germany. Even though I could speak French and Spanish, the only language we all had in common was English, so we chatted all night in broken English. Everyone got along with each other and felt somehow connected. This simple camaraderie was a microcosm of how I wanted the world to be where people share and communicate from the heart despite cultural differences.

The train to Stonehenge stopped overnight in Canterbury. It was very cold, and too late to get any lodging, so I was forced to stay on the station platform. It is quite remarkable who you meet at 2:00 a.m. on a station platform. That night I met a young man just a year younger than me who had been shot in his chest by friendly fire in the British Territorial Reserve Army where he was training as a soldier to help put him through school. His injury made him question what was important in life because he wanted to do so much more before he died. His story really had an impact on me and made me reflect about how I wanted to live and what I wanted to do with my life. I realized how blessed I am that my parents could always pay for my education and any trips I wanted to take. I always assumed that life was so much better in Europe. I took my awesome country, Canada, and my amazing family for granted.

Later that morning, at Stonehenge, as I sat in the centre of that prehistoric monument on the ground with others watching that magical dawn, I felt a sense of powerful spiritual energy and a deep connection to planet Earth. Watching the sunrise over the horizon past the rolling green hills of Stonehenge, I had a strong urge to connect with my spiritual centre. Where better to do that than head to Rome, the centre of my religion, to try to find my life path.

BE PREPARED

I wanted to see everything Italy had to offer, so I traveled on sleeper trains overnight to save on accommodation; this also allowed me to see more of the countries that I was going through. The European trains are like traveling hostels: cramped rooms with strangers sleeping on bunk beds and sharing bathrooms.

Besides night trains, I slept wherever I could—in train stations, on park benches, and in one town, even in a police station! By then it was August, the month when Western Europeans go on vacation to their neighbouring countries and book up all of the hotels, motels and hostels. I was on my way to Assisi and there was no ongoing train in the rural town where I stopped. The station was closed for the night and I had no accommodation because at that time I never planned anything in advance. As I was wandering the town, I decided to put my Italian language skills to the test and speak with the police to check if there was anywhere to sleep. In response, they asked if I wanted to sleep in the jail cell. It was like something out of a Western movie—a little shack for the police station with one cell that you could see from the front door. I laughed and asked them if they were joking. They said that it was the safest place in town and they would leave the cell door open so that I wouldn't feel like a criminal. Finally better sense prevailed and, being stranded, I eventually agreed. The best part of the experience was that in the morning the police even had a fresh cup of cappuccino for me.

The biggest lesson from that experience was that I needed to be more responsible, plan ahead, and not just fly by the seat of my pants. Being spontaneous is good, but a little preparation goes a long way and ensures you don't end up in jail!

MY SPIRITUAL PATH

Ironically, it wasn't in the Vatican City where the Pope presided or the Sistine Chapel that I felt closer to God and found my inner peace. It was on another night I'll never forget, when I was stranded (again!) with no train in some small forgettable Italian town at 4:00 a.m. There was a homeless man in front of the train station and all he asked me for was some toothpaste. I remember sharing my toothpaste and water while he shared his story with me. He used to be a salesman for his own kitchen supply company that went bankrupt and he ended up on the street because he had no family. He took me to a construction site and said that I would be safe to sleep there. I thanked him and offered him money, but he wouldn't take it, so I gave him my toothpaste and he shuffled off down the street. I cried thinking that he could be like my grandfather, and it made me realize how having family and friends to support you in tough times is such a precious gift. I thanked God for the blessing of my family and friends in my life. In reality, I knew that I would never truly be able to understand what homelessness was from just one night. However, it opened my eyes to life's challenges and made me so grateful for my life and good fortune. I will never forget that homeless old man and my experience that night.

Next, I traveled to Pisa, Bologna, Lucca, and Verona where I wanted to see the opera, *Aida,* performed in the Verona Arena. Typical of me, once again I arrived too late to find any accommodation. So, as I wandered the empty dark streets at 2:00 a.m., an older man who looked like a gangster from Al Capone's era or from a Humphrey Bogart film walked out of the night mist toward me. He was wearing a black pin-striped suit and a black fedora. I should have been scared, but for some reason I wasn't. He asked me if I needed somewhere to stay; he said that it wasn't safe for a young lady to be alone on the street at that time of night. He requested that I follow him, and we eventually arrived at a big wooden door attached to a really high, thick wall surrounding a large area. He knocked on the door very loudly with the metal door knocker and a few minutes later a nun appeared. I suddenly felt this huge wave of relief come over me—as it turned out, the convent doubled as a hostel for young women. I turned back to thank the man again, but he had vanished back into the mist. I felt that he was an angelic godsend, and that night I thanked God for protecting me. That realization of being loved and protected by a higher power in the universe I have kept with me ever since. A strange sensation of wholeness started to enter the void of restlessness and aimless wandering that had resided in my heart for so long.

My final stop on my way back to France was Venice. I love costumes and dressing up, so I just had to buy a mask from Venice. I found some spare change to take the ferry from Venice City to Lido Island, my favourite part of the city. I swam in the warm salt water of the Mediterranean Sea and felt instantly at home. Gazing at the cityscape from across the water, I understood why so many painters and artists were inspired by such a beautiful view. Unexpectedly, a wave of great sadness touched me as I realized my time in Europe had come to an end. Yet, a wonderful serenity and satisfaction came over me. I felt healed and complete again. I would be able to handle the next stage of my life, whatever it was.

REFLECTING

At 20 years old, I had traveled to many different places and had amazing experiences and met some incredible people that allowed me to build up my previously broken spirit. My belief and trust in God and my faith in humanity were restored, I had reconnected with nature and Mother Earth, and I had proven to myself that I didn't need to live by others' opinions of me. I have learned how to view my past positively, and realize that there will always be those who will try to bring me down, but I am strong enough to stand on my own two feet. On my travels, I discovered as long as I keep praying to God, he will direct me on the right path, and that my gratitude for my family, my friends, my life and the Earth will keep me strong and I cannot go wrong.

Currently, I am home in Canada and my next adventure is to study for my master's degree in music and musical theatre performance at NYU. Since that time in Europe when I was 20, my journey has taken me to this point where I know my path and what I am supposed to do here on Earth. To those 20-year-olds out there, from the sum of my life experience, I say, follow your heart. Be humble; try not to be egotistical and self-serving by finding a way to use your talents, intellect, skills and creativity to serve others. In doing so, you will find peace, happiness, purpose, and love.

STEPHANIE

Who are you? What does life have in store for you? Some of you may have it all figured out. Most of you don't have a clue! I can tell you that it doesn't matter to which group you belong because you have plenty of time to work it out. In this moment, you may have more questions than answers, but you also have all the power to define the answers. If you are one of those people who has a plan for your life, then you may believe that you already know the answers. But I can assure you that life is guaranteed to throw you a few curve balls. As I have navigated my way through life, I have learned a few things that have kept me sane when, for all intents and purposes, I should have gone absolutely nuts.

Who I am and who I continue to grow to be is a result of my trials and my tests. My story begins in a housing project in Ohio and unfolded there for 18 years. Often you hear people giving schoolteachers credit for changing their lives, and for me this was absolutely the case. I actually had two teachers who recognized something in me that I hadn't recognized in myself. They recommended me for a program designed for intellectually gifted children. Now, I don't know if you know what that really means but what it meant for me was that I was a "nerd" who lived in the hood! That scenario brought about a whole set of challenges for which I was not prepared. In my "gifted" classes, it was usual to have these group projects to be worked on outside of school. Well, I was the only African American in these classes with upper class white kids, who in my mind lived in mansions and were filthy rich. I was terrified for them to find out where I lived. So I would have them drop me off at my grandmother's house all the way across town, wait for them to leave and walk home. While they were at home on their computers, completing the papers that were required to be typed, double-spaced in 12-point font, I was walking to the library past the drug dealers and addicts to type mine.

I struggled tremendously with where I fit. In one world, I had really good friends who went to school whenever they decided and never thought about college. In the other world, the primary topic of conversation was going to college. It was never even a question of whether or not they were going. The conversations were in regards to which one they were going to. I had no idea how I would get to college. We had no money for that. I started to learn through this internal struggle of living in both of these worlds that I needed to get laser focused on what I wanted for me. I needed to shift my focus from external—what my friends thought—to internal—what did I really want for myself? I really wanted a college degree. I felt more than anything in the world that a degree would be my ticket to the life I wanted. As I look back, I know now that my struggle trying to fit into these two worlds was because I was not aware of my worth. Being aware of what you bring to every situation will ensure that no one can tell you what you're worth. It takes away the need to fit in. This technique of understanding your worth prevents you from getting caught up in other people's definition of you.

Friends, family, love interests, co-workers, and even strangers passing on the street all have a point of view about you. The more you let those perceptions define who you are, the easier it is to get lost and distracted. You have to know and be confident in what you bring. It may not be, and should not be, what someone else brings. You have something unique, something that no one else has. Maybe it's a skill, maybe it's a talent, maybe it's your personality or maybe it's your smile. You have to know without a shadow of a doubt that there is something that only you bring to every situation.

The other side of this is being aware of your opportunity areas and where you can build and acquire new lessons. The best way to do this is by conducting an "internal audit." Can you be a better friend? Can you be a better daughter or son? As much as you should not let others define you, you should also listen to how you impact other people, and the sweet spot is finding the balance between being who you are while bringing the best of you to others. In this stage of discovering my self-worth, I decided that I was going to resist peer pressure, not care what people thought about me, and nothing and no one was going to keep me from my dream. It sounds like I had figured it all out, huh? Wrong! My senior year in high school, I got pregnant. The friends in my neighborhood were like, "I knew you weren't all that" and the friends in my "gifted" classes were whispering and snickering. I wasn't as strong and focused as I thought I had become. I had failed. I had failed myself and sabotaged my own dreams.

I didn't know it, but this was the foundation for the building of another sanity-saving technique. I learned to allow myself to fail and to forgive myself for it. You will fail. You will fail over and over again. But the greatest lessons and the seeds of success come from failing. I am completely convinced that a person who has never failed at anything doesn't know much of anything. If you have never failed at anything, you have no idea of your potential because you are not stretching yourself beyond your comfort level. Don't beat up on yourself and don't allow others to beat up on you for failing. Take pleasure in the courage of trying and try something else. How can you ever discover your passion and purpose on this planet if you worry about failing? You should work to develop a "get your butt off your shoulders" attitude and try it again. You owe it to yourself and to the world to uncover your gifts, and this can only be done through trial and error. So I got my butt off my shoulders and figured out my next steps. I learned to adapt.

I am sure you have heard the phrase that the only constant thing in life is change. There have not been truer words spoken. Those who are most successful at navigating this life are those who master the art of adaptability. It is very easy to lose sight and get thrown off balance when things don't go the way you expect. This world can make you crazy and you can often feel that you have taken all you can bear. It is in these moments that the ability to adapt can keep you balanced. How you get to your goal is important, but it can come via many routes. Each route comes with a new and different lesson to be learned. So if one route takes you to a dead end, then adapt your path! Find another route to your goal. If someone disappoints you, then they taught you something about them that you didn't know. If you don't get into the graduate school of your dreams, then you learned something about that school. So adjust your plan and take another route. The last thing you should do is get derailed. Mastering this technique definitely takes some practice, and often some heartache, but it is a tool that will virtually guarantee your success. Luck favors the prepared. So when you are thinking of what you want for yourself, prepare alternate routes. Approach every situation with a willingness to adapt if and when it becomes necessary.

In my case, I had applied to and been accepted at four universities: Howard University in Washington, DC, Hampton University in Virginia, Syracuse University in New York, and last on my list as a local option was Miami University in Oxford, Ohio. So I started at Miami University in Oxford when I was seven months pregnant. At first, I was the pregnant girl on campus, and then I was the girl on campus with the baby.

It was during those years that I truly discovered the pieces of who I am and this is where my strength was really activated. I had a lot of rough times and nothing about going to college with a baby was easy. There were countless times I wanted to give up; I carried a full course load and worked full time. I remember being dead tired, driving to class and parking my black Plymouth Medallion that I had bought at an auction between a Range Rover and BMW and feeling so defeated. But moments like those were defining moments in my life. Those were the moments that I used as motivation to finish. And I did finish. I finished in four years and went on to obtain an MBA.

In no way did I accomplish any of this on my own. My situation forced me to enlist the help of others, and it was at this point that I learned the benefit of creating an inner circle. In my experience, this inner circle should include peers, but mostly people who are older and smarter than you. This is your motivational power source. This circle is where you can always be your truest, most authentic self without judgment; but you will get guidance. Your inner circle can be leveraged as a sounding board for ideas, serve as a professional network, give relationship advice and many other things.

I find that this select group of special people can bring a tremendous amount of perspective to your journey. It's great to have a mentor, but a team is even better; it gives you a continuous source of support. You should ask people you admire to be a part of your power team. They don't even have to know about one another. The other advantage to this is that you will begin to notice that you eventually become someone that these people look to for your perspective and input. It will become a reciprocal relationship. They will look to you to provide the younger, cooler perspective in their journey. Having the opportunity to draw from my inner circle was integral to my accomplishment of graduating from college and being able to acquire my post graduate degree.

At this point in my journey I thought I had succeeded and all was right in the universe. But because life is never calm or quiet for long, I continued to experience things that brought about new challenges.

When I was growing up, my father had been married to someone other than my mother and had other children. I always felt like an outsider. For many years, I was the secret child that no one was supposed to know about and that weighed extremely heavy on my confidence. How could any man be okay with nurturing and loving all of his kids except one? What was wrong with me? Why wasn't I good enough to have him be proud of me too? I was my mother's only child and there were so many times growing up that I felt so alone. When I was 26 years old, I discovered that the man I had worked so hard to impress and to win his love was not my biological father. Unfortunately, he had passed away long before I learned about this, so I will never know if that was the reason I felt so left out.

During this same time, I also discovered that my biological dad knew that I was his child and had made a conscious decision to not be a part of my life. So, in my mind, this was yet another person for whom I was not good enough. I was defining myself using my interpretation of what I meant or didn't mean to other people; so much so, that I found myself in an abusive relationship, telling myself that it was because of something that I had done and that I needed to make it better. I didn't even realize that I was perpetuating this cycle of trying to be validated. I was trying to be good enough.

It was deep in this dark place that I came to understand how little I knew about myself. I decided to take personal inventory and embark on the tough task of opening up and examining my soul. I needed to figure out what was keeping me in this miserable place. It was in this space that I discovered that none of what I was going through or anything in my past defined who I was. I learned to listen, truly listen. I listened to my heart and found that my definition of me was mine and mine alone to craft.

Listening is very different from hearing. While hearing is the process of sound vibrating against your eardrums, listening is internalizing and feeling what is meant from the words you are hearing and the emotions you are experiencing. This is a skill that requires practice, emotional maturity, self-awareness, and the desire to improve. The earlier you master this skill, the sooner you control your own destiny.

I know that when I was in my twenties I talked way more than I listened, but somewhere along the way life made me shut up. It was at this point that I got significantly better at navigating this journey. I could be more courageous and self-assured because I was truly equipped with a different level of knowledge. You can take what you hear and digest how and if you should apply it to your life. I felt like I was hearing everything for the first time (because I really was). Not to be too dramatic, but when you learn the art of listening, it's like an awakening. It's a rebirth of all the preaching and lectures that you have been getting from parents and teachers your whole life. But now instead of it sounding like Charlie Brown's mother (waa waa waa), some of it—most of it—makes sense!

By truly leveraging all the sanity-saving techniques I have described, I solidified my value and self-worth; I set standards for myself and others in my life. This gave me permission to feel that I deserved to be in a better physical, emotional, and mental place. I am definitely still a work in progress; none of us is perfect nor should we expect perfection from ourselves. Every day is a day that I work to fine tune my techniques. The journey to get to my current place was a hell of a ride and the journey continues.

As for me, at the youthful age of 38, life definitely feels new. Every day I learn something about myself. Some days are harder than others, but I genuinely like who I am. For a long time my identity was defined by others, but in this moment I feel courageous and free. I still have some holes to fill and some rocky places to make smooth, but overall I am closer to happy than I have ever been. This journey has been a roller coaster of emotion. There have been days when I cry over the littlest things and then there are days spent laughing out loud. My advice to you is to be unique, start positive trends and most of all, live in YOUR truth. And when you face a difficult situation, thank the universe for loving you enough to teach you something.

What I want you to take from my story is that you are already equipped with everything you need to be whatever you want to be. You are already blessed with your gifts and your purpose. You only need to learn how to activate it. Take the time to learn who you are and who you want to be.

Your journey is also a process of trial and error; but remember that failure is only a lesson in how to be better on the next try. Now that I am in my thirties, I find that reflecting on all the drama in my life has helped me to be confident and determined in dealing with all the new drama that is bound to come. Every day is a new journey, but my view of the journey is very different now. There is really no end to anything, only new beginnings.

We are all more vulnerable when we are going through something. When we are in the middle of a trial or a test, it can be very hard to see the bright side. Have you ever noticed that when you are depressed or you don't feel well that it continues to get worse unless you get out of the house or find something to occupy your time? That is because when you are alone and isolated, it is easier for you to convince yourself that you can't make it through, that you should be depressed, that the universe doesn't see you or hear you. But it is in these times that we define our future. It is in these times that if we trust the universe, we are making deposits for our future.

If we accept the trial, we can learn something from it, something we can use to be successful in the future. Use your trials and your tests to make you different, to set you apart from everyone else around you; your trials become your advantage. Because of your personal test, you know something that no one else does. Through your trials, you develop resilience. Resilience is the ability to come through adversity and come through it better than you were before. Expect trials, expect tests, and you won't ever be ambushed by the unexpected. You can navigate any circumstance or situation. We all make mistakes. But I don't care how far you fall; you have the power not only to be restored but to be set apart.

Wishing you love, laughter and— Peace of Mind!

TERRI

A few months ago, a very close friend was giving a speech on my behalf. It was my wedding day, and my maid of honor, Picot, was standing in front of my closest friends and family talking about me. For as long as I can remember, I have avoided being the center of attention because I didn't feel like I deserved it; but it's one of those things you can't easily escape on your wedding day. My nerves were starting to get the best of me, and I nervously started sipping the wine I was holding. Then I heard my dear friend tell some of the most beautiful stories, and the people around the room were smiling affectionately. This was the first time I had heard my own stories from another perspective and I realized it wasn't shameful at all. On a day where we were celebrating love, success wasn't defined by achievements; rather, success was described as happiness. I didn't just arrive at happy; it was a culmination of choices that led me to my mid-thirties, a collection of passports full of stamps, an even bigger collection of friends around the world and a partner to travel the world with as we grow old(er).

For a long time, I had this idea that life followed a simple progression, and if I followed this plan then I would be happy, just like everyone else. It seemed easy enough; go to high school, then university, then get a job, get married, have kids, work work work, then retire and start enjoying free time before kicking the bucket. Sound familiar? I can't remember the exact age that it developed as my view, but I do remember a writing project in high school where I had to write about where I saw myself in ten years.

This was likely a common assignment for teachers to give seniors in high school. I would guess that the teacher who assigned this project read many essays over the years, and they were probably all pretty similar. I wrote about how I would already be married, with children, and have a successful career as a securities trader in New York City. The house, the car, the job and all the details were all defined. I may have even named the kids. My ten-year vision wasn't clearly developed, as it was all about ME (I was only 17 after all). My career, my children, my house, and no mention about what kind of person my partner was, or what role he would play in my life. It was as if I had taken a picture of my future family, but the lens was only focused on me and everything else was blurry and out of focus. Everything was in the picture, but 17-year-old me wasn't paying any attention to anything except her.

I handed in the essay and, to be honest, I never thought I would be reflecting on it so many years later. It has been about 19 years since I wrote about where I saw myself in ten years, and the reality couldn't be further from my initial vision. Without any regrets, I have reinvented my vision to include a much brighter and more enlightened present and future. I have widened the lens and now there is a much more animated picture.

Not everyone has a ten-year plan when they are 17 years old; or 25, for that matter. I certainly did not have a clear plan. I made a lot of choices in my teens without really knowing where I wanted to end up, which meant I spent a lot of time in my twenties backtracking. At the end of high school or the end of university, there are so many crucial decisions to be made, and sometimes we make the wrong choice and are not satisfied with the outcomes. This was the case for me. When I reflected on some of the choices I had made, I was not satisfied with the outcomes. In order to fix this, I had to take a few steps back in order to move forward.

The first symbolic decision for me was the decision to go to university. Not many people will tell you that going to university was a bad choice, but for me, it was. I didn't know what I wanted to do or what I wanted to study. I knew what others told me I should do and what I should study, but when I got there, nothing felt right. It took two long years for me to realize that I didn't want to be there, and didn't want to do this. So, I transferred schools until I found the right fit. Third time was the charm, and I ended up studying business management just to get the degree done and dusted. A lot of time and money would have been saved if someone had told me that it is OK if you don't know what you want to do right after high school. Not everyone should go to university right after high school. University is usually used as a steppingstone where you learn, grow and train for a career or industry; however it can be counterproductive if you don't know which industry you want to train for, or even what direction you are headed.

Once I completed my bachelor's degree, and before I started my career in finance, I rewarded myself with a trip I had always dreamed of and went backpacking around Europe on my own for a few months. That summer was about finding myself, and what I found wasn't exactly what I expected. It forced me out of my comfort zone and put me into challenging situations. I had very little money, didn't know anyone, but was having the time of my life. I met interesting characters, immersed myself into new cultures and discovered I was more adventurous than even I thought. I met a lot of recent university graduates, but more people that had just finished high school and were taking a year to travel before returning home to attend university. Everyone I met had a different reason for traveling, and everyone had amazing stories about where they had been, what they left behind, and what they were looking forward to when they returned home. There was one guy who was traveling around the world on his bicycle for a few years, for no other reason than to see the world and be able to say he'd done it!

I had a six-week itinerary planned which included five countries, but at the four-week mark I knew it wasn't enough and I wanted to see more. I started off in England, and went to Ireland next. I was less than two weeks into my journey, and still had

France, Spain and Italy to come, but the thought of returning home in only four more weeks and not seeing Greece, or Holland or the Czech Republic was weighing on me. I extended my trip a number of times and took a few spontaneous excursions that made the trip more memorable simply because I hadn't planned it for months. Visiting the Topkapi Palace in Istanbul and Checkpoint Charlie in Berlin, riding a bicycle in Amsterdam, going to jazz clubs in Czech Republic, eating fresh seafood while island hopping in Greece, pub crawls wearing only a toga in Rome, and sleeping in a creepy old hostel near Edinburgh Castle during the tattoo festival were just a few of the escapades that I am so glad I didn't pass up. After three months and 13 gorgeous countries later, I finally returned home with every intention of going back to Europe, keeping in touch with all my new friends and planning reunions.

Back in New York it was time to execute my plan. With a bit more life experience under my belt, I made some mature choices and was ready to follow my career path. After a few years on this road, I had all the material things that one might think defined success. I lived in NYC, had a good job in the finance industry and was beginning to see my ten-year plan through. Only trouble was, it was not my definition of success. That familiar feeling, the uneasy feeling of discomfort, started to show its face once again. How can this be? Isn't this the plan? So, naturally, I ignored it. But, like a nagging toothache, it didn't go away until I finally addressed it. I thought about it for another six months, but I still wasn't sure what I wanted to do. I knew I had some expensive hobbies, like travel, and interests that needed funding some way or another; plus, I had to pay back those student loans from my degree. This was one of the hardest choices I had ever been faced with. Do I stay in the job even though I am not happy, or do I leave to pursue something else? What if I regret it? What if I want to get my job back? I felt like giving up would make me weak—until I finally let go. Letting go was the strongest and most empowering feeling I had ever experienced.

I chose to pursue another career and was forced to start back at the beginning, but I was happy to do it. This time I had an end goal in mind, a new career to work towards, and a plan, a real plan that made sense. A fresh start meant a lot of work, but I was up for the challenge because I wanted to find something I could do that would make me happy. I went back to university and completed my master's degree in education.

By the time I finished, I was about ten years from when I wrote that essay in high school, and I hadn't achieved any of my objectives. There was no relationship to mention, let alone a husband and children. There was no career, no home, just a new degree and so many choices to make in order to find my way, again. At that moment, I certainly wasn't focused on achieving anything from my previous ten-year plan. My concentration was on defining new goals, and making new plans. I had an opportunity to redefine everything, not just my career.

At this point in my life, when my focus was less on the tangible outcome, I started making more positive choices, the kind that would lead me to a much happier lifestyle. My goal was to be happy, but I hadn't defined how to achieve it. All I knew was that I wanted to make a difference. Not necessarily a saving-the-world kind of difference, but at least to feel a sense of reward from the kind of work I was doing. This reward didn't have a dollar sign in front of it like my previous career, but instead had a thank you, or sometimes a big hug or even an innocent young smile. Education has been the most fulfilling career, and a choice I have never regretted.

Once again, I rewarded myself for all the hard work of a completed degree and hit the road; this time I planned to be away for three months. I headed to New Zealand and Australia on my own. I may have had a few doubts before I headed to Europe, but I was full of nothing but confidence and excitement before I left for New Zealand. I made it from the tip of the North Island to the end of the South Island, climbing mountains, bungee jumping from bridges, white water rafting, taking bone carving lessons and private Haka lessons from a Maori Chief. I even made it to tiny Stewart Island, which is a tiny piece of heaven that most Kiwis never journey to as it's so remote and off the beaten track. If you asked me at the time, I would have said I would probably never make it back to Stewart Island.

Traveling and having a break between all the demanding work and study before jumping into a full-time career was really beneficial. I had some time to think about what would come next. Not everyone needs to travel in order to escape or relax, but it was clear to me I thrived while traveling, making connections with people and with places, and experiencing something not available in New York.

I had met one guy who was attempting to break the world record for circumnavigating the globe in a boat; this was so unlike my friends and family in New York who didn't leave the tri-state area more than once a year. It was this man who first put the thought into my head that I should move to New Zealand to teach. He joked about how the Kiwi kids would get a kick out of my New York accent, and I should find myself a good Kiwi bloke to settle down with.

My mind was clear and focused and I started to stress at the thought of my trip coming to an end. I had to make some more mature choices, so instead of extending my trip, I returned home with a plan that would satisfy my need for adventure while also pursuing a career.

I chose to make a total change. I was embarking on a new career; why not make an even bigger adventure out of it? I was hoping to combine my new career with that feeling I felt when I traveled through Europe and New Zealand and Australia, the exhilaration of travel. I traveled to Thailand and took part in a teacher-training course at a Buddhist monastery, along with 60 other teachers-in-training. At some point, you will reflect on important times of your life, and hopefully some moments will stand out as significant. This is one of my standouts. I learned so much from the dynamic group of people I was teaching with, and I learned even more about myself. Immersed in a new land, new culture, and learning from the most amazing students (the monks) I was out of my comfort zone once again, but I was enjoying every moment. I felt an overwhelming sense of peace—finally!

This diverse group of people from all over the world and all walks of life had one thing in common: a sense of adventure which we all shared and was the reason we were all so far from home. I had done a lot of travel prior to Thailand, but this was the first time making a foreign country my home. It was a powerful feeling to be surrounded by like-minded travelers.

While living in Thailand, I took every opportunity to travel, meet new people and try myriad different things. There were batik painting classes, mountain climbing, ten-hour-long journeys on dodgy buses just to get to a beach for the weekend, English camps, sliding down waterfalls, surfing on beautiful beaches, making friends with monks, learning new languages and cultures, trying new and interesting food at night markets. It was always a risk not knowing what it was, but most times was the most delicious; my favourite, though, was the sticky rice and ice cream.

A friend of mine, Picot, and I lived in a traditional Thai house with a giant six-foot monitor lizard living in the backyard, and an equally scary yet smaller lizard living in the guest room. There were the cobra snakes in another house I lived in with a group of French boys who screamed louder than me, and the monkeys that would come up to you on the street and steal your snacks. It was experiences like these that I began to cherish over material objects, and favoured memories over souvenirs. My bank account was nearly empty, but I felt rich beyond my dreams.

I loved living in Thailand, but found myself longing for something new, something different. One of the greatest benefits of teaching is that there are opportunities all over the world, so I wasn't confined to one city, or one country. When I began to look for a new job outside of Thailand, I was like a kid in a candy store. There were jobs offered in all kinds of exotic places and I wanted to go try all of them out. I had ants in my pants and couldn't stay put any longer. I decided to leave Thailand, but I wasn't heading home. I chose to move to the United Arab Emirates.

I'd been to a lot of places and had so many amazing experiences up until this point, I couldn't even begin to imagine what to expect from a move to Abu Dhabi. My eyes were wide open taking in the beautiful scenes of the desert and modern cityscapes, and while I was working in a local school, I had an insight into the culture. This was the most challenging job I ever had, but it forced me to work harder and improve my teaching skills. Although there were many times I wanted to leave, I chose to stay and step up to the challenge.

I am so glad I decided to stay in Abu Dhabi. I never could have seen it coming, but a chance encounter with a handsome man, someone even more adventurous than me, and I was swept off my feet. This was the easiest choice I ever had to make. I had been swept off my feet before, but each time I ended up heartbroken and sobbing. But when Travis called and asked me on a date, without hesitation I said yes. I wasn't going to miss out on getting to know this guy. Our first date was the most proper, most memorable, most awesome day of my life (until our wedding day). We had brunch at a gorgeous restaurant, flew in a seaplane over The World Islands and around the world's tallest building, had drinks at a royal palace; and just when I thought nothing could top the first date, on our second date he cooked dinner and serenaded me with his guitar after a day on the beach. There was a moment during the second date when I took a step back to look around, and I realized I was happier than at any other point in my life. I was in love!

All of a sudden, I was including him in my plans, and sharing my dreams with him. We were making plans to travel together, build houses together and even planned to adopt a dog. When Travis was offered a job in Hong Kong, we were faced with making a tough decision. Do I stay in the Emirates, or go to Hong Kong? This was a choice we made together. It was a few years in the making, but it feels like I blinked my eyes, and we were making ten-year, 20-year and longer-term plans together, and designing our happily ever after. We now live in Hong Kong with our two dogs, Rocky and Chardonnay. Now when we plan a vacation, we think about friends and family we have all around the world, and whom we can go visit.

A few years after I met the man in New Zealand who was circumnavigating the globe, I saw him again on TV campaigning to save the whales. We still stay in touch, and I was so happy to share with him the news that I did finally find myself a nice Kiwi bloke whose family lives on Stewart Island. I have returned to the tiny island several times and enjoy it more and more each time.

It has been almost 20 years since writing that essay in high school, and I've learned a few important lessons along the way. The experiences you have in your late teens and early twenties, the people you meet or the connections you make can be essential to your journey.

Some of the most important decisions in your life will require a lot of reflection, but this is not the only time when self-reflection can be beneficial. As you reach milestones, take a moment to look back and decide if this is still what you want, if this is still what makes you happy.

I didn't know how big an impact my trip to Europe would be, and didn't know that I could do anything other than finance. Have the courage and the confidence to let go if need be, because if you are strong enough to let go, then you are definitely strong enough to pick yourself back up again.

Enjoy the journey.

TOSH

At the age of 33, I found myself sitting in a New York City Hilton Hotel ballroom with 28 communication professionals from around the world. This was my first meeting as a US district representative to the International Board of the International Association of Business Communicators (IABC). As I listened to the insightful and intelligent dialogue that took place throughout the first four hours of the two-day agenda, I couldn't help but question, "How did I earn a seat at this table?"

Our lunch break gave my mind a rest from trying to keep up with the overwhelming amount of detail and the intimidating wealth of knowledge that seemed to flow with ease from all of the board members, except me. As I quietly waited to join the rest of the board members at the lunch buffet, Marcia, a board member I had met at one of the association's conferences approached me.

"So, what do you think of your first International Board meetings?" she asked. "You've been so quiet."

"It's very interesting," I replied, "and everyone seems to be so much more informed on the issues and raise intelligent points that contribute to the conversations. I just don't have anything more to contribute."

Marcia looked me straight in the eyes and said, "Speak up, because you have something to say."

Wisdom comes when you least expect it, and when you're most in need. The challenge is recognizing and doing something with wisdom when it comes. At 33 years old, many people may have already given up on thinking their lives can be different. For me, Marcia's willingness to take the time to check in with me and offer these eight words changed my thinking and experiences as I continued to serve on the Board, as well as how I designed my future—personally and professionally.

QUIET OBEDIENCE

To better understand the impact of Marcia's words, it's important to understand where I came from.

My family has a Japanese heritage, and ended up in Utah after being relocated during World War II from their homes in Tacoma, Washington to the Tule Lake War Relocation Center, California. My grandparents—like many of their friends—demonstrated their loyalty to the United States by quietly accepting their circumstances and believing that everything would work out in the end.

"We were just farmers," my grandfather told my dad and his brothers and sisters. "There's nothing and no one left from our past." They never questioned, never spoke about their life in Washington, never spoke of family who still lived in Japan, and never blamed the war or relocation for what could have been. They avoided anything that would draw attention to themselves. They respected authority by never questioning or contradicting.

My parents inherited the same thinking. They followed without question or criticism the path that their circumstances afforded them. They got good grades in school. They attended church every Sunday—which is where they met. After graduating, Mom went to work while Dad served in the US Army. My sister was born in Germany where my father was stationed, and then they returned to Ogden, where my younger sister and I were born.

Like my grandparents, my parents melted into conformity, avoided drawing attention to themselves, and respected authority. They successfully created a good life for our family. We didn't always get what we wanted, but we had what we needed. The example they set for me and my sisters confirmed that quiet obedience works.

Of course, as all good parents do, Mom and Dad had high hopes for me and my sisters. But I don't think they had anything specific in mind. We were given the freedom, support, and encouragement to figure it out for ourselves. Quiet obedience doesn't lend itself to many options.

FOLLOW INSTRUCTIONS, STAY OUT OF TROUBLE, AND STUDY HARD

Throughout grammar, middle, and high school I was fortunate to maintain good grades. Quiet obedience taught me to follow instructions, stay out of trouble, and study hard. Unfortunately, with this mentality I created for myself additional pressures and failed to build confidence in my own voice. Three examples occurred in my fourth, fifth, and ninth years.

When I was in the fourth grade, my teacher decided that she would manage some of the trouble students by moving them to the desks at the front of the classroom. This meant that since I was one of the better students, I was moved to a desk in the last row. The problem was that my eyesight had changed and I couldn't read my teacher's writing when she wrote on the board. But, I didn't say anything because that would have questioned my teacher's authority. After several months of struggling with my studies and it starting to reflect in my grades, my teacher called my parents in to discuss the sudden change in my performance.

My parents returned home and informed me of the reason behind the meeting. I explained that I was moved to the back of the classroom and I couldn't read the board during classroom lectures or to copy assignments.

"Why didn't you tell your teacher that you couldn't see the board?" Mom asked me.

"Because my teacher needed to put the kids who weren't doing well closer to her." And I perceived my move to the back of the classroom as recognition of being a good student.

My parents took me to get my eyes checked, and that's when I started wearing glasses. My teacher apologized for causing problems for me, and I stayed in my desk at the back of the room.

The next year, our class had decided to profile the music of Stephen Foster for our annual program. My teacher wanted to leverage my artistic abilities by having me draw pictures depicting various moments in Stephen Foster's life. The pictures were converted to slides that we projected behind my classmates' singing and recitations.

Creating these drawings was no small task. And this work was in addition to my regular studies, which my parents noticed by the increased amount of homework I had to complete every night and over weekends. I explained to my parents the cause of the increased workload, and they contacted my teacher to let her know that this situation was unacceptable.

Of course, I didn't want to complain about the additional work because my complaints would contradict my teacher's vision, and would let down my classmates. And the honor of being given this task was my teacher's way of recognizing my artistic abilities.

My last example comes at the end of ninth grade, when the principal announced my classmates, Tina and Cliff as the class valedictorians. Although I was very happy for Tina and Cliff, I was a bit surprised by the announcement because the class rankings indicated that the first and second rankings belonged to Tina and me. Rather than questioning the announcement, I concluded for myself that there was some other calculation beyond the rankings that determined the valedictorians.

A week later I was called to the principal's office. The first thing that I could think of was "What have I done wrong?"—An interesting response from someone who hadn't ever been called to the principal's office. The principal informed me that there was an error in announcing the class valedictorians, and asked for my forgiveness. Upon reviewing the class rankings, Tina and I would be the class valedictorians.

This was the first time I had to write and present a speech in front of an audience, drawing attention to myself, and expressing my opinions. After 15 years of living a quiet obedient life, it wasn't very comfortable completing this task, but I did as I was told.

SOMETIMES WE CAN'T SEE THE ANSWERS THAT ARE STARING US IN THE FACE

Throughout high school, I continued to earn good grades, and prepared myself for university. But I knew that getting accepted to university would take more than good grades. I had to get involved in extracurricular activities to demonstrate a range of interests and social skills. Overall, I would say that my high school experience was average—nothing that I would classify as unique or out of the ordinary.

After graduation, the majority of my high school friends attended a local university, which allowed them to continue living in their parents' homes and stay connected to each other. I had developed an interest in the sciences during high school, and decided to attend the University of Utah where I could establish my path on a career in medicine. This was a significant move for me because I was leaving my family, friends, and familiar activities to start my self-discovery.

Being away from friends and family forced me to explore options that I may not have known were available to me if I had stayed local. Joining a social organization, getting involved in student government, and volunteering in the community helped me realize how much of a "small town" life I had lived. During my junior year, I was selected to participate in a new approach to freshman orientation in which 12 student advisors were trained to take groups of eight to ten freshmen through registration, campus resources and activities, and a campus tour.

At the time, I wondered how different my university experience would have been if the student advisor program was in place when I was a freshman. Perhaps with the guidance of a student advisor, I would have had a better plan of attack. By this time, I had changed my focus from medicine to law, changed my major four times, and was starting my fifth year. Not the smoothest journey.

But now that I think back on my summer as student advisor, I realize that without my not-so-perfect journey, I wouldn't have been able to give firsthand advice to help reduce the incoming freshmen's fears and anxieties:

- You don't have to have all the answers now.
- Don't be afraid to change paths mid-stream.
- Take time to explore your options so you may discover and pursue your true passions.

Sharing these messages every day for several weeks helped me internalize my own advice. By this time, I had accepted that it was all right to not have all the answers. I seemed to be doing okay despite changing paths several times. But I was still struggling with the passion piece. Having bought into quiet obedience for 22 years, expressing passion wasn't an easy thing to do. To complicate things further during my senior year, I was given the opportunity to serve as a prosecutor for the campus social societies. The worst thing that could happen, happened—I hated it.

Graduating from university wouldn't be followed by law school, but it was time to makes some decisions.

WE ARE OUR OWN WORST CRITICS

Observers of my life would likely describe it very differently from my "reality." Would anyone describe me as a chronic introvert or socially awkward? Would they indicate my extreme insecurities about my appearance, intelligence, and abilities? And would they interpret my years of quiet obedience as a positive or negative quality?

A few years after graduating from university, I had one of those "what I want to be when I grow up" conversations with my younger sister. She was a bit annoyed with my self-pity and said she and our older sister referred to me as "the golden child." As the only son of three children, she said, "For Mom and Dad, you can do no wrong."

"You've done a lot of things, and made a lot of decisions that were questionable," she explained, "but in the end everything always worked out." Mom and Dad would discuss their concerns about my decisions and actions with my sisters, but they never discussed them with me. From their perspectives, quiet and obedient wouldn't be the words they would choose to describe me. It appeared to my sisters and parents that I spoke my mind, challenged norms, and approached life with a well-planned and orchestrated path for success.

SPEAK UP, BECAUSE YOU HAVE SOMETHING TO SAY

They likely believed that my plan included joining IABC. In reality, this was a necessity because I had been given a job opportunity to create a new public relations function. Although my bachelor's degree was in communication, it was in argumentation and negotiation, not public relations. I needed quick access to tools, templates and best practices.

I had learned while at university that one of the best ways to explore and develop skills and gain hands-on experience is through volunteering. So, I volunteered for the local chapter board. As I had hoped, my IABC membership and volunteer work put me in contact with a lot of great people who were willing to share tools, templates and advice that I could immediately apply to my job. And within a few years, I was offered new jobs with increasing authority and responsibilities. I had stumbled into a career that I really enjoyed and could see a future of continued growth and learning.

Having gained so much from my IABC experience, I continued to accept leadership roles, which advanced from the local level, to the western US region, to the International Executive Board and Marcia's advice during my first International Board meeting.

I took Marcia's advice to heart and started speaking up. It didn't happen overnight, but over time I gained the confidence to speak up during International Board meetings, at work, and within the community. Seven years later, I was elected to serve as IABC's International Chair. I returned to school to obtain my master's degree, which lead to an offer to join the faculty as an associate professor. And my career has continued to provide me with challenging and rewarding experiences.

Marcia's advice provided the motivation for me to internalize the advice that I had given to incoming freshmen so many years ago:

- You don't have to have all the answers now;
- don't be afraid to change paths mid-stream; and
- take time to explore your options so you may discover and pursue your true passions.

And as you navigate your life journey, **speak up, because you have something to say.**

SUMMARY

In reading these personal stories there are several themes that emerge. The most pervasive theme alluded to is "follow your heart." Some variant of this concept was central in everyone's journey. Some people knew who they were meant to be at very young ages; for others it took time to figure out. Some people were always true to their heart, others repressed feelings for years until they found the courage to live their truth. However, for every contributor, in order to find true happiness and success they had to follow their own path in life and make decisions based on their own unique passions.

In a related motif, contributors often spoke of the fear associated with following your heart. It takes audacity and bravery to take the path less traveled. Sometimes following your heart is risky, but with these risks come rewards. Authors often spoke of the "good fear" of doing something new and challenging, and the resulting satisfaction and strength that comes from following through.

That's not to say things will always go well. Another consistent theme in the stories was that the path to fulfillment is not straightforward. Life will throw you curve balls. You will make mistakes. What's important is that you adapt to the changes that come your way, and that you forgive yourself and learn from the errors you make. Often it's your attitude and perspective that differentiates a negative and a positive experience.

It helps to have tools and the proper frame of mind to manage life's challenges and opportunities. Along this vein, contributors often spoke of the importance of hard work, planning and learning. Hard work is productive use of time to achieve something, not to be confused with the sense of struggle that may be felt when you're in a situation that doesn't feel right. Planning is described by one contributor as the element that moves a dream into the realm of reality. While some situations require detailed planning, it is important not to forget, as one contributor advises, to "leave white space" in your plans. Leave room for the unexpected things that may come into your life.

Learning is a continual process that contributors considered essential, but it meant different things to different people. Some stressed the importance of a formal education, while others spoke of the disconnect they felt within the education system. Learning may also be obtained through experiences (like travel), through self-reflection (using journals or internal audits) or via mentors (for career and life advice).

This illustrates the differences that appear in the contributors' stories. For example, some contributors speak of family as a support system for their life's journey, while others experienced family as a barrier to making authentic, non-traditional choices. Some found happiness through travel, while others found happiness by settling down. While some contributors highlighted the need for certain selfishness in living an authentic life, others highlighted the importance of service to others to obtain a sense of fulfillment. Differences don't indicate conflict, but rather highlight the variation and uniqueness of each journey.

As a parting thought, it's important to address the role of confidence. How exactly do you find the courage to follow your heart? We live in a society where self-esteem is perceived as something parents give to children with the right parenting style, or turned on in people via positive affirmations. These stories show that confidence comes from listening to your inner voice, taking the risk to follow your heart and learning lessons along the way until you truly understand that you are unique, strong and capable of accomplishing your dreams (with a little hard work and planning).

Best of luck on your journey!

BIOS

ALMA KENUP

Although Alma's home state of California claims a huge chunk of her heart, as soon as she could she left the comforts of the US to follow her love of different cultures and languages. Along the way, she learned Portuguese, Arabic, French and Spanish. After flitting about the world for a few years, she decided to settle with her husband (whom she met abroad) in the United Arab Emirates. There she gets to be part of the world's largest educational reform where she teaches kindergarten. Alma is passionate about helping children love learning. She believes that as children's first encounter with the educational system, she should strive to make the experience as wonderful, magical, fun and enriching as possible. Alma chose to participate in The20Project because she would like to inspire others to explore their world.

AMBERLEY LAVERICK

Everyone has a story so unique and singular in all the kinks and curls it travels upon. The20Project has been an opportunity for Amberley to share hers whilst also encouraging her to reflect. So it has been one part storytelling, one part personal development.

As an educator, Amberley looks for different ways to 'do' education. This has led her to working across cultures, age groups and countries. Writing creatively, however, is where she feels most productive. Not just her own writing, but providing space for people to create and share their own words. She believes that we all have a story and a voice.

In the future she hopes to develop programs where people, no matter their background, can come together to tell their tales. It is in this sharing that Amberley feels we are connected, in a way that enables barriers and prejudices to be challenged.

Currently, Amberley is supporting Martha Chumo in the growth of Nairobi Dev School, a web development program in Kenya. They are aiming to make the school economically sustainable so that it can continue to offer fully funded scholarships to students. Quite possibly, she is the only person to have lived in Kenya as an ex-pat and not seen an elephant.

This perfectly describes Amberley's ability to miss the obvious yet notice the obscure. She has no permanent address right now as she writes the next chapter of her story.

DAVE MITCHELL

Dave Mitchell lives and works as a business manager in the United Arab Emirates and is totally committed to life as a roving expatriate. Seven years abroad have given him a wonderful opportunity to travel, meet and live with some extraordinary people from around the globe.

In his previous life, he grew up in small town New South Wales, Australia and it came as quite a shock when asked by his friend Hilary to contribute to The20Project. There are many others with incredible achievements to offer that Hilary could have called upon.

Hopefully, his slightly different views on life may resonate with young people who are finding their way and are maybe not at ease with the world's general expectations of success and happiness. The experience of contributing to a project such as this, with an emphasis on providing advice to youngsters in their twenties, is a daunting one, and one that requires a certain amount of introspection and self analysis. That doesn't come easily, but perhaps his story may strike a chord with some readers.

His great loves and passions in life are travel, photography and diving and not necessarily in that order. A successful career, wealth and stability are not particularly on his list of necessities.

As he heads into his sixth decade, he is rapidly readjusting his goals and will soon be heading down a very different pathway into a world that allows the pursuit of passions that matter to him. Hopefully, that will be a story worthy of the 30 Project.

You can find his work at: https://www.facebook.com/davemitchellimages

FLAVIO KENUP

Originally from Brazil, Flavio was inspired to learn about the world after taking a series of short trips on motor scooter in South America. Flavio is currently participating in a Jiu-Jitsu program with public schools in the emirate of Abu Dhabi, in the United Arab Emirates. There he works as a school supervisor, overseeing the daily operations of Jiu-Jitsu instructors in their various school facilities. He is happy to work with some world-renowned competitors in a sport that is a passion of his.

Favio chose to participate in The20Project because of his belief in the importance to share stories that are different from the general narrative. No one ever says to a young person, "An option would be to follow your gut and take huge risks." But that's what he believes should be shared.

HEATHER STAFFORD

Being creative is one of Heather's passions, so she is glad to have had the opportunity to participate with The20Project. Knowing from an early age that being an entrepreneur is what she is meant to do, Heather previously owned a salon and day spa. She currently works full-time as an executive assistant while also running her own small business (GeminiRed Creations) which consists of blogging, affiliate marketing and making handcrafted items.

Heather is in the process of designing her first iPhone app with the help of a young developer. Her goal is help him develop his entrepreneurship skills while also producing an app that many people will enjoy.

Collaborating on The20Project is Heather's first published work outside of blogging. She has written two books that she plans to publish after she finds the right illustrator.

HILARY A. CURRY

Hilary founded The20Project in January of 2014, and through her international connections brought together the project contributors. The20Project has been an amazing opportunity to work with some very inspirational people, and she hopes that the project helps others to navigate their own life journey.

Currently living in North Vancouver, Canada, Hilary is a management consultant working in the field of change management. She recently switched over from working for the large firms to find her tribe at PeopleFirm LLC.

One of Hilary's goals is lifelong learning. In 2015 she is taking on the challenge of her PhD Human and Organizational Systems at Fielding Graduate University in Santa Barbara. Her goal is to complete her degree with a practical tool that will help organizations with their challenges related to Cross Cultural Change Management.

When she is not studying or working, Hilary can be found underwater, on top of a mountain or on an adventure somewhere in the world with her camera, you can check out her work at http://www.halstonphotography.com.

JUAN M. RODRIGUEZ

Juan is an entomologist working in Saudi Aramco Oil Company located in Saudi Arabia. Juan holds a Bachelor of Science in entomology from Texas A&M University and an MBA from the University of Phoenix online program. He is currently pursuing his MSc in entomology from the University of Nebraska. Juan is also a veteran of the United States Air Force.

Having grown up in the small town of Magnolia, Texas, Juan's professional career has taken him to various locations throughout the southeastern US: Mississippi, Georgia, Arkansas and Florida. Since 2008, he has been living in the Middle East, UAE and currently in Saudi Arabia. Juan also speaks English, Spanish, Russian and Arabic.

His passion for traveling has grown since living abroad, and he has traveled to more than 30 countries, each time appreciating and embracing the cultural differences. He has never visited a country he did not like. Juan also enjoys photography, diving and attending jazz concerts.

Juan's successful journey in both his personal and professional life is a result of maintaining a positive attitude along with other attributes he has applied. He believes that these principles, when adopted at an early age, can help individuals become successful. That is why he feels The20Project is a great opportunity to share his experiences.

JULIA KERRIGAN

The20Project is so intriguing to Julia because she often feels that she is not so far away from being 20 herself. Since it's been such a wild ride, she wants to share what's shaped the first decade of her foray into adulthood and to connect with others who have a similar desire.

Her first reaction to learning about The20Project was that her current life is nothing like what she predicted it would be at 20; her second was that she had to be part of it. Once she started writing she realized that a lot of the lessons she learned in her early twenties are just as applicable as she approaches 30.

Julia has a tendency to move around a lot, but after living in four cities in four years she currently makes her home in a tiny condo on the west end of Toronto with two roommates (her fiancé and ten-pound Havansese puppy). She thinks she'll stay around for a while.

Julia is still not sure what she wants to be when she grows up, but currently helps executives at a bank get the development opportunities they need to be great at what they do. She equates what she likes about her current and previous jobs with her passion for helping people achieve greatness.

Beyond writing for The20Project, training her tiny dog and making her urban condo feel like a cottage, Julia spends her time exploring the neighbourhoods of her new city, especially those with great brunch.

MARGARET EBRECHT

The20Project is a very exciting opportunity to share life experiences and lessons with someone just starting their life adventure. It provided Margaret with the chance to reflect and focus on what was most important to her decision-making and the significant turning points that shifted her direction in both her career and personal life. The most important aspect of Margaret's life that has guided her is the saying, "Do what you love" and you will find that everything else will fall into place.

Currently, Margaret lives in Deep Cove, North Vancouver, British Columbia in a wonderful waterfront property. For the past five years, she has been working for a large commercial real estate firm in the project management corporate global services area. For the previous 25 years, Margaret has worked as a consultant to various corporate, government, and institutional clients, focusing primarily on project management, strategic planning, technology implementation and change management.

She enjoys travelling, swimming in the ocean, surrounding herself with anything white, and creatively expressing herself with mixed media and fibre art.

MICHELLE ARDUINI

Michelle is a 30-year-old PADI Divemaster, with dual degrees in British history and English literature, and has spent the last decade figuring out what she wants to be when she grows up.

Born and raised in North Vancouver, BC, Canada, she has called six different countries home in the last eight years. Previous careers include running a daycare, working at a bank, bookkeeping for a multi-million dollar construction development company and driving a tractor. Most recently seen leading underwater scuba diving tours in the Aegean and living on yet another Greek island, she is coming to the (possible) end of a nearly four-year travel stint that has taken her from the depths of the Great Barrier Reef to the top of Kilimanjaro, the sandy deserts of the Empty Quarter and the rice paddies of Bali.

Michelle jumped at the chance to be a part of The20Project so that she could share the broad experiences of her twenties with others who might be looking for a bit of direction; and to prove that sometimes the best direction is none at all!

Michelle has been chronicling her travels of the last decade on her blog The Travelling Twin (www.thetravellingtwin.com) and updates it regularly with pictures, videos, and posts about her life as a working traveller. And yes, she is a twin! With options abounding for the 20-somethings of today, Michelle hopes that by sharing her experiences she can encourage others to take a chance on their futures and venture off the beaten path.

NANCY-JEAN LAHN

There are moments in life that seem to be driven by kismet, and the opportunity to participate in The20Project was just that for Nancy-Jean Lahn. At a crossroads in her life, The20Project allowed her to reflect on her journey and hopefully provide insights for those in similar situations. This experience has shown her that, while she may not have all the answers, sometimes simply asking the questions is enough.

Growing up in rural town of Hanover, Ontario, Nancy-Jean's parents instilled the belief that learning was the key to improvement, so she went to The University of Western Ontario and graduated with an honours degree in English, Anthropology. In order to learn more Nancy-Jean attended Humber College's Public Relations program and upon completion worked in the marketing and fundraising fields specializing in not-for-profit organizations and event planning. Never losing sight of her true passion, she applied and was accepted to teacher's college.

Presently, Nancy-Jean is a high school English, drama and special education teacher who strives to engage and inspire her students to achieve their own personal best. Having experienced firsthand the difference a teacher can make, she hopes to be able to return this kindness as often as possible.

A self-proclaimed musical theatre geek, in her spare time she can be found performing on stage, helping out backstage or directing student productions. Nancy-Jean is also proud to be a member and featured soloist for concert choirs in the area.

NICOLA HOLDEN

When Hilary said she was looking for contributors for The20Project, Nicola jumped at the opportunity. She felt that sharing her life story, and the convoluted route she took to find a career she loves, could inspire others just starting out on their own career path. With the benefit of hindsight, Nicola has realised how important it is to choose a job that you can do with your heart.

Her upbringing in Zimbabwe was one of privilege that brought her to London, where she now lives. Initially qualifying as an engineer, Nicola now has her own interior design business, Nicola Holden Designs. She feels very fortunate to have a vocation that she feels passionate about.

Nicola is very aware that so many other people don't have the opportunities that she has had along the way, and she feels honoured to be a trustee for Makomborero, a charity that gives underprivileged children in Zimbabwe some of the same opportunities that she took for granted.

When Nicola is not creating beautiful homes for other people, or sharing her passion for Zimbabwe's children, she can often be found in remote corners of the globe, discovering new cultures, people and places, exploring nature's beauty, and adding new birds to her life list!

ROBERT JAQUES

Looking back on his life and career, Rob realized that many of the pivotal moments or decisions had come about because of someone's advice, whether it was Bill the pipefitter taking him by the shoulder and saying, "Come along, young fella; let's go see another engineering f*** up!" or Catherine the labour relations consultant who told him, "I'm going to tell you this and you won't believe me, but ten years from now you'll find me and tell me I was right. For every hour of meeting time, you need ten hours of preparation time." (For the record, it didn't take ten years. She was right and Rob told her that in less than two months.) He had learned a lot from people who just gave advice, with no expectation of payback, so when Hilary asked, he jumped at the opportunity.

Born in Saskatoon, Saskatchewan, Rob grew up in Calgary, Alberta with a short stint in Sydney, New South Wales. After graduating with a degree in engineering, he lived in Fort Nelson and Fort St. John in BC, Calgary, and London, Ontario. For the last 11 years, he has lived in Orange County, California with his wife and two children. With over 20 years as a management consultant working in the oil and gas, transit, and healthcare industries, it's a bit of a strange mix, but funny enough, it all seems to work together.

Rob is currently working on the emotional upheaval caused by his son graduating high school and going off to college.

RUSSELL CULLINGWORTH

Russell Cullingworth was born a fourth-generation South African with family roots in West Yorkshire, UK. As the youngest of five children in a liberal English-speaking family, he had an enjoyable childhood despite the country's racial difficulties during the apartheid era. In 1980, his family moved to East London on the South East Coast of South Africa, the city that Russell refers to as his home town. After school, in the absence of better options, he decided to follow the advice his family to enter the accounting profession, which is where his story really starts.

In 2009, while working at Canuck Place Children's Hospice, Russell had an epiphany that caused him to leave accounting in search of a career where he could work with and inspire others. He discovered a particular passion for working with young adults, helping them to understand themselves before making critical life choices. As a young man in both marriage and career, this lack of understanding had caused him to portray himself not as he really was, but as someone he had come to believe he should be. In 2010 he became fascinated by the link between Emotional Intelligence (EQ) and psychological preference and co-found founded the Centre of Excellence for Young Adults (ceya.ca). In 2012 Russell incorporated EQAdvantage Learning and Development Inc. and in 2014 founded EQinLove.com. Russell was remarried in 2013; he and his wife, Christine have a great passion for helping others to develop the four pillars of EQ— self-awareness, self-management, social awareness and social management—as they believe that these hold the keys to success for everyone.

SANDIE ATKINSON

Sandie Atkinson was born in Adelaide, South Australia, grew up in Waterloo, Ontario, and landed in Vancouver 24 years ago. In between, she travelled and worked for two years in Australia, and then backpacked through South East Asia and Europe in her early twenties. As her story states, she met her Vancouver-born and bred husband in Australia, and they enjoyed travelling together prior to their marriage.

Since 1994, Sandie has been with EY in Vancouver as a project coordinator. She is a member of the National Brand, Marketing and Communication team. She manages the EY Entrepreneur Of The Year program in the Pacific region, as well as being the national program manager for the EY Entrepreneurial Winning Women program. She finds her work very satisfying through daily interactions with sponsors, EY leadership and entrepreneurs that come through the program.

Each day, Sandie and her husband come home to their most rewarding role as parents to three children and one golden doodle, named Maddie. They have two teenaged boys, and one girl who is 10 going on 20! With three children, there are many opportunities to reflect on being on the other side of 20, and she finds lots of time to share her thoughts and offer great advice to her children, although they often don't realize it at the time. When not spending time with her children, you can find Sandie on or in the water. A self-professed water baby, she swims regularly and loves paddle boarding at Deep Cove in North Vancouver. She is also an amateur cellist, an avid reader and her home is filled with lots of photos of family vacations and fond memories.

SÉBASTIEN LACOUR

Sébastien is a management consultant, and received a BSc (Hons) from Trinity College in Dublin, an MBA from Grenoble Graduate School of Business and is also certified PMP by the Project Management Institute. As a specialist in digital marketing, social media, crowdsourcing and knowledge management, he found The20Project to be an excellent opportunity to share experiences and help future generations to save time and accomplish their dreams.

After having spent most of his time in Europe and travelling in North America, Africa, Asia and Oceania, he is now settled down in one of the most beautiful countries of South America—Colombia—until life and his actions take him somewhere else, or not. As well as consulting to help companies to improve their bottom line, he is also a trader, investing on the major Indices such as the CAC 40, Dow 30, DAX, Nikkei and ASX 200. The trading activities provide him the opportunity to work around the clock and full autonomy in relation to customers and other business activities. This whole independence ensures full integrity and objectivity when handling projects as consultant.

Sébastien is also passionate about sports. He has practiced Aikido-Iaido for 11 years and reached the Shodan level; he has climbed most of the French and Swiss Alps summits; and since moving to Colombia he has also undertaken Wushu and horseback riding. Thanks to the Caribbean coast of Colombia he can also continue diving in the tropical sea, where he spent a lot of time while in Martinique.

As an anti-conformist, Sébastien is always ready to confront ideas and propose disruptive ways of thinking. His goal is to challenge the mainstream and give people the opportunity to think for themselves. Lately he is working on a start-up to promote online business in Colombia. He can be contacted at http://www.sflacour.com.

SHANNON TEEMULL

Shannon Mara Teemull is a singer, actor, dancer, writer, singer/songwriter, director, teacher and linguist currently living and working in Toronto, Canada. She was born in Montreal, Canada to parents from Trinidad and Tobago, and has one older brother. She grew up in Saudi Arabia in an American gated community, and returned to Canada for high school and university.

After earning a Joint Specialist Honours Bachelor of Arts Degree in French and Spanish with minors in music and drama at University of Toronto, Shannon went on to complete a three-year Diploma of Performing Arts at Randolph Academy for the Performing Arts. She intends on going to New York University to complete her Master's Degree in Music and Musical Theatre Performance in 2015.

In addition, Shannon also holds the CELTA certificate for English Language Teaching to adults from University of Cambridge, and has lived in Paris, France, Sienna, Italy, Guadalajara, Mexico and London, England.

Shannon strives to use her art to address social issues and to convey the message of love. She thanks God, her loving family and amazing friends for all of the many blessings she has received in her life. She truly believes in the power of positive thinking, education, life experience, faith, hope and above all spreading love. She is thrilled to be a part of The20Project.

STEPHANIE ALEXANDER

Stephanie is from Hamilton, Ohio, USA. Professionally, Stephanie spent the last six years as a consumer insights manager with Procter & Gamble in the Global Feminine Care business where she was responsible for identifying new market opportunities with sizeable and distinct consumer segments. She was also responsible for designing and executing research for consumer testing in North America and Western Europe. Most recently, Stephanie accepted a position as a senior customer account executive for Hormel Foods.

Stephanie earned a BA from Miami University where she double majored in sociology and Black world studies and minored in criminology. In 2005, Stephanie obtained her MBA. She has a passion for mentorship and leadership training and is the founder of ASPIRE, a non-profit focused on the personal development and empowerment of girls ages 14 to 18. Stephanie also has a passion for baking and runs a small bakery (Georgia's Sweets) out of her home.

Stephanie has three children and a pet chinchilla who serve as her motivation to continue to grow and prosper. She is in the process of getting to happy—determining what really makes that happen, deciphering authenticity from perception, and finding the courage to live in HER own happy. Life has definitely been a roller coaster and Stephanie's path is far from traditional, but she feels that it is hers to own. She is still a work in progress but has found the space in her spirit that makes her comfortable doing things on her own terms. She believes that her thirties have been a period of self-discovery that is both enlightening and liberating.

TERRI TAIAROA

Terri Taiaroa (Lyons) grew up in Putnam Valley, New York, the suburbs of NYC, where both her mother and father worked in the finance industry. Her first job at 16 years old was a summer internship at a small security trading firm. Every summer until college graduation (Pace University was where she earned her degree, but she attended Mount St. Mary's University and SUNY Purchase as well) was spent working in similar firms, then she started a full-time career at Jefferies & Company where she started out in the Compliance Department before moving onto the International Equities trading desk. At the height of her career, Terri lived in Manhattan but was burning the candle at both ends and quickly burnt out.

Terri left her job at Jefferies and returned to the familiar halls of Pace University where she earned a master's degree in teaching, childhood education. While earning the degree, Terri held multiple jobs, but refused to return to finance. She worked in a deli, taught at a rough (not sure how else to describe it) middle/high school and then worked at a golf shop, all of which she enjoyed far more than her stressed-out life as an equities trader.

The day after completing her master's degree, Terri flew to New Zealand and has been traveling since. Currently, she is a primary school teacher and certified nutrition advisor living on Lantau Island in Hong Kong with her husband, Travis, and two dogs, Rocky and Chardonnay.

Terri views teaching as a passion, not just a career. Teaching is not exclusive to classrooms; all it takes is for one to inspire others. Terri wanted to be a part of The20Project in order to inspire others to take their time, figure out what they want, and never be afraid to leave one thing in order to pursue true happiness.

TODD "TOSH" HATTORI

Tosh spent 20 years of his life creating and leading communication programs that helped organizations connect with their diverse audiences. You'd think that writing one chapter about life experiences would be easy for a professional communicator. But he emphatically stated "this is one of the hardest pieces I've ever written. Good communicators are 'behind the scenes,' writing about other people and their circumstances. Writing about myself is definitely a specialized skill that I don't have."

Tosh recently made a dramatic change in his career by joining PeopleFirm, LLC., as an organizational performance consultant, helping good companies become great. Making this change was a demonstration of one of his life principles: continuous learning, growth, and development.

He also credits his volunteer leadership roles with the International Association of Business Communicators (IABC) with expanding his cultural horizons. As with his teaching experience, he believes he gained much more knowledge and experience than what he offered through speeches and presentations.

Tosh (a shortened version of Toshiharu, the Japanese name given to him by his Hattori grandparents) lives in Seattle, WA with his partner, Stephen, and their Weimaraner, Winston. He spends his free time running—mostly on a treadmill given the frequent Seattle rain, reading novels, and creating a variety of things that allow him to apply his creativity.

www.the20project.com

www.ingramcontent.com/pod-product-compliance
Lightning Source LLC
Chambersburg PA
CBHW070453120726
47910CB00003B/1028

* 9 7 8 0 9 9 3 8 8 7 6 2 8 *